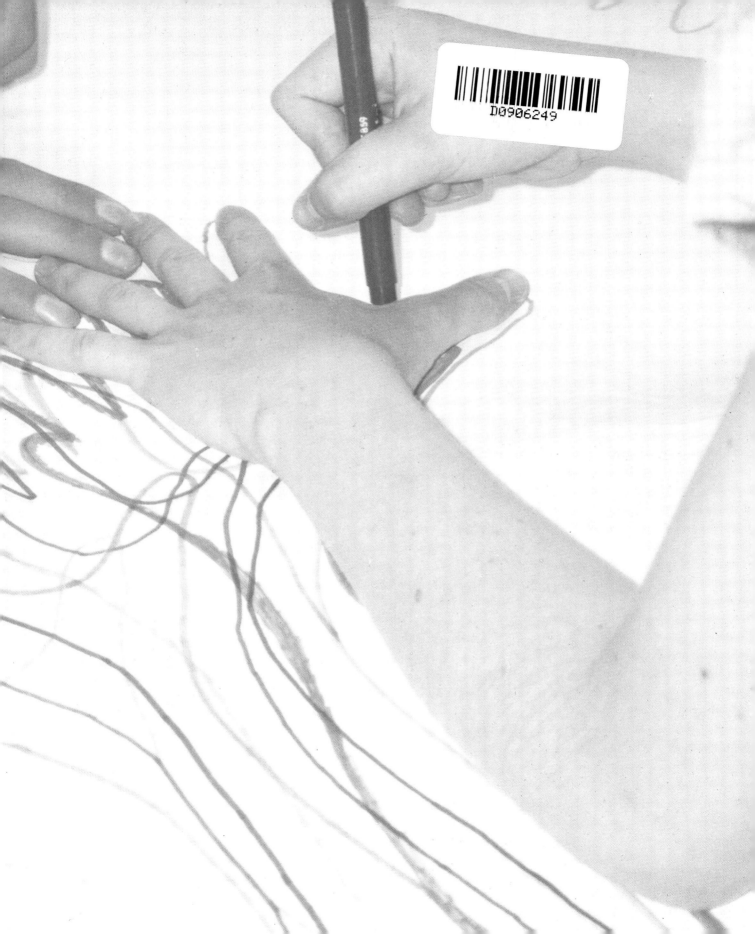

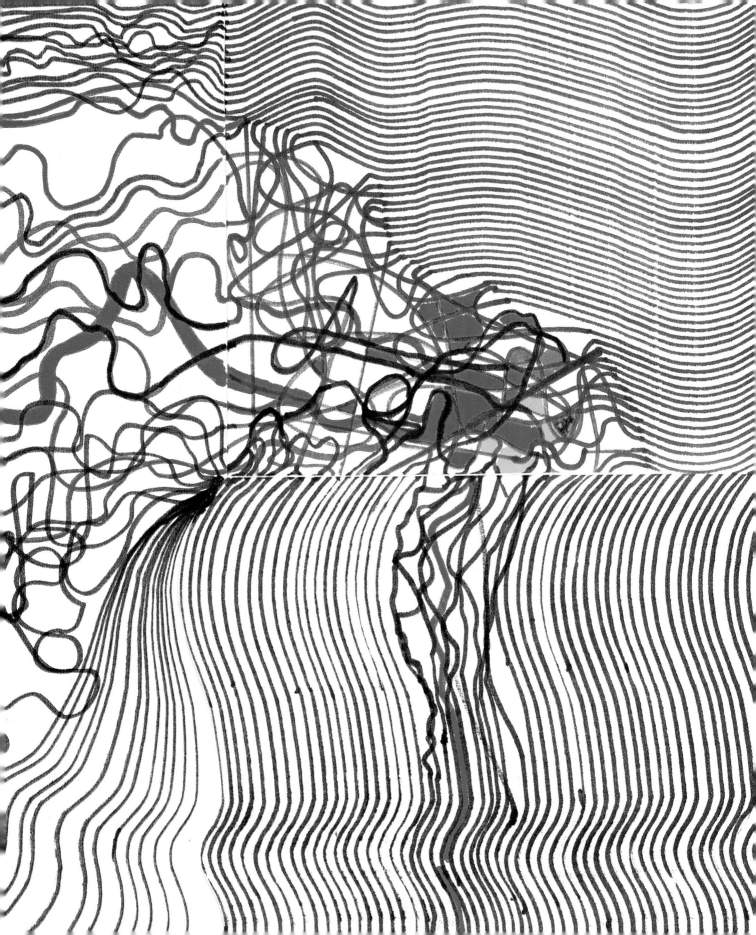

Teaching Children to Draw

Written by Karla Cikánová

CRAFTSMAN HOUSE

Designed and produced by Aventinum Publishing House, Prague, Czech Republic
First published in the English language in 1992 by Craftsman House
Reprinted 1997
Distributed in Australia by Craftsman House,
Tower A, 112 Talavera Road, North Ryde,
NSW 2113, Australia

in association with G+B Arts International:
Australia, Canada, China, France, Germany, India,
Japan, Luxembourg, Malaysia, The Netherlands,
Russia, Singapore, Switzerland, United Kingdom,
United States of America

ISBN 976 8097 12 4

Written by Karla Cikánová
Translated by Alena Linhartová
Illustrations by children from the school in Londýnská Street, Prague
Instructive drawings and photographs by Vladimír Rocman
Graphic design by Vladimír Rocman

Typeset and printed in the Czech Republic, Prague
1/99/41/51-02

11025602

Contents

Preface

Here are some ten-year-olds' answers to the question: Why do you draw?

I draw because it enables me to express better than in words what I'm thinking about, and what I feel . . . I like to draw my own fantasy world. Adults should find time to draw, too, as they could forget their worries, and return to their childhood, and understand us, children, better . . . Drawing is fantastic, to know how to do it, or even if you cannot do it. What matters is that I want to draw, and enjoy drawing . . . I like to sketch various objects and animals, in order that I may learn more about them . . . I can express in a drawing feelings of sadness or happiness; or remind myself of somebody . . . I draw because I want to know more clearly how I comprehend the world.

When I was searching for a motto for this book, I could not find anything more appropriate than the children's answers quoted above. If we read these statements once more, and think about their wider implications, we might summarise them as follows: 'Through creative expression children convey their little disappointments and pleasures; they respond rationally and emotionally to the world in all its variations and forms; they are seeking their place in it; they make friends with the world; they become acquainted with and even re-create its mysteries; they discover in their own good time its inner logic and connections. Using creative activities children are able to move from the real world to the imaginary world, and thus increase their perception of everyday reality. Children seem to have their model of concrete reality embedded in their own mind's eye.'

This book shows how an adult might encourage and develop the child's perceptiveness and awareness of the surrounding world. Simultaneously, the adult can support the child's natural inclination to discover for himself, and to be creative. The subject matter of the book is based on the fundamentals of human relationships: the child and the world of people; the world of Nature and objects; the world of technology; and the world of writing. This book attempts to develop an awareness and a deeper understanding of the creative nature of lines, and of the content which is being conveyed through creative expression. The book should serve primarily as an inspiration, not as a set of prescriptions to be copied mechanically. Children may use an exaggeration, a certain form of writing, or a certain tool in order to express what they know about reality, how it affects them and what images or associations it evokes, without resorting simply to copying reality.

Each chapter is followed by so-called 'Mini-gallery'. This comprises less familiar pictures of Nature and 'artificial' Nature, and works of art which are loosely connected with the subject matter of the respective chapter. They might provide an inspiration for children's creative perception, and also be a preparation for what children might discover in Nature or in galleries. They do not represent a rationale, or the 'only possible' explanation of how to appreciate and understand a natural shape or a work of art. They might assist in finding out whether children

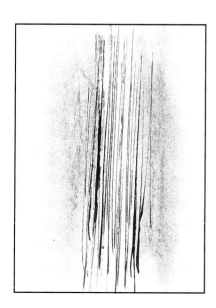

are able to think about the wider implications of Nature, or the impression given by a work of art; whether they are able to discern in this dialogue any personal and even human links.

Any creative activity has its deeper human subtext. A creative expression can surely portray the world, though primarily as it is perceived and understood by a person. Thirty thousand years ago the first hominid did not differentiate himself from other creatures by communicating (dolphins can communicate, too), or by using tools (chimpanzees can also use tools). Primitive man differentiated himself from other creatures by drawing signs and pictures in caves. He might have drawn in order to make himself less frightened; to understand, to identify and explain himself; or to make all pervasive Nature favour him. Should this ritual, in a somewhat changed form, not be upheld today? Should we, together with our children, not get to know and appreciate Nature more sensitively, and ourselves too, through variously inspired creative activities? In this way we might become attuned to Nature with all its natural harmony! Let us hope, at least, that anyone who, through creative activity, continues a dialogue with his friend – be it a tree, a stream, a stone, or a butterfly – will not harm his friend.

1

1

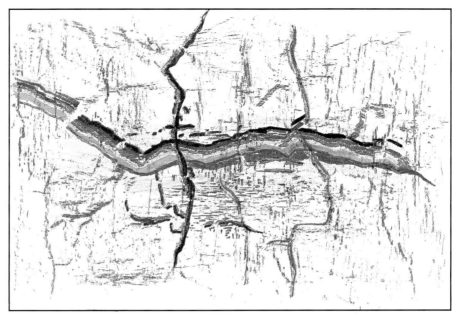

2

The Pleasures of Play

Discovering graphic expression. Exploring lines by rubbing and drawing with thread, comb, brush and sponge. The variety of marks made by a block of wood. A collection of lines – the tool determining the line produced.

1 *A restless line* has occupied the area in a unique manner. It was produced by a thin piece of string dipped in white paint, using various movements, such as rolling or wiggling. This is just playing and discovering what the line can express and how varied it can 'appear'.

2 *The wall rubbing.* Children discovered the lines which had been 'captured' in random cracks of a wall, and they explored them by rubbing. They reinforced the most important horizontal and vertical lines by drawing over them in a coloured pastel (further illustrations and instructive examples on pages 12–13).

Lines and their resulting structures arouse the attention of the amateur artist or observer only insofar as they faithfully reproduce material reality i.e. the model of a drawing. Is an apple 'correctly' shaped or shaded? Is the portrait of a person a good likeness of that individual? However, a drawing taken in this way seems to exclude the artist's ability to select consciously different lines which, by their subtlety or depth, may tell more about the fundamental basis of reality. It is, indeed, possible to express and thus differentiate, by different lines, stillness or excitement; happiness or sadness; whether in a portrait or a landscape.

The line itself is a marvellous organism which only exists for us as a flat surface area, but as such does not exist in the objective world. Observe, for example, how reverently a small child regards the line in his first 'scrawl'. The child creates this scrawl and talks to it: 'He barks like a dog' when producing a strong zig-zag line, or 'He squeals like a frightened mouse' when a fine line

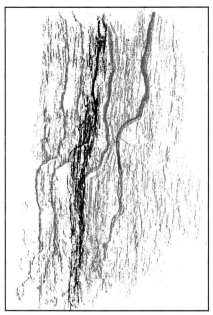

3

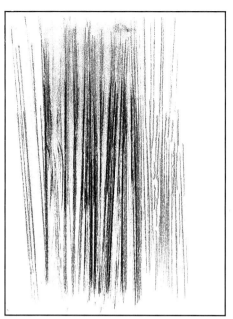

4

3, 4, 5, 6, 7 *Rubbings* of knotted nylon thread, jar lids, spaghetti, a small block of wood, or a cracked coat of oil paint were creatively finished by the children. They tried to increase the number of lines; to complete them, and change their colour. They also drew the lines in pencil or charcoal, and simplified their drawings until they produced a form of sign (illustration 7).

When rendering cracks in plaster it is necessary to press a thinner sheet of paper tightly to the plaster, using the left hand. Firstly, the children rubbed oil pastel or chalk over the entire surface in one direction only. The number of lines can be increased in an interesting variety by shifting or turning the paper.

is involved. The finished drawing represents an adventure for the child. The child is able to evoke a mood of good or evil; stillness or noise.

The creative activities involved in drawing may become livelier and more varied if in the beginning we offer children simple games of discovery in which unfamiliar tools are used (e.g. a comb or brush). Children learn that lines have many different shapes and speak in different languages, too. Lines have their individual characteristics and moods like people. We will say more about this in Chapter Two.

Now, let us offer children the fascinating adventure of discovering lines with the help of the graphic technique known as *rubbing.* Rubbing is the technique of rendering, on paper, the uneven surfaces of objects by applying pressure from above.

Let us take children out for a walk. During the walk we might speak about mysterious, enchanted lines, for example in cracked walls, which are waiting for somebody to come and free them. We can also tell children that Leonardo

5

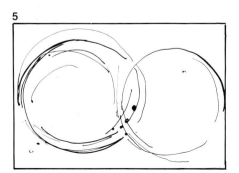

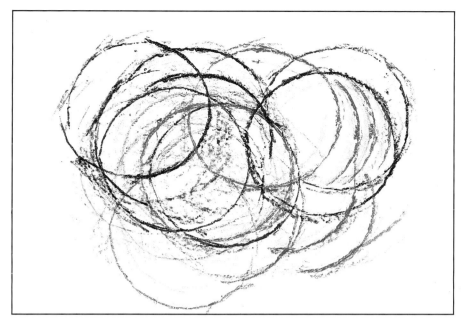

6

da Vinci, the famous Renaissance painter and man of science, noted that the composition of a painting could be greatly inspired by looking at cracks in old walls. Obviously, one must be able to see and feel creatively. However, for the moment, we are just discovering lines with children. They will, doubtless, be interested to learn that the technique of rubbing was already known in China over two thousand years ago. Nowadays, this technique is commonly used by archaeologists as it is a speedy and precise method of recording the uneven surfaces of historical artefacts. Graphic artists also use the technique of rubbing in their work.

7

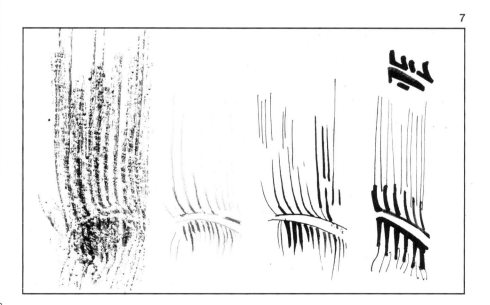

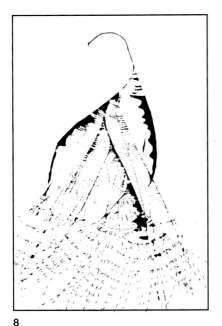

8   9

We soon find that children are very creative and enthusiastic in their 'hunt' for various lines to rub. They can arrange and label their collections, for example, 'rubbings from my room', 'rubbings from the garage', 'rubbings from our street'. Their collections can also be classified according to the materials used – rubbings of thread creations which suddenly appear when 'rubbing' textiles (sack cloth, strings); rubbings of patterned netting (woven baskets, mats); and rubbings of natural objects (the structure of wood – the annual rings, stones, stalks). Rubbings can be developed further by cutting and arranging, and adding drawings to them (see the following chapters).

8, 9, 10, 11 Children might like to dip a piece of wet, thicker thread half-way into a shallow bowl which contains Indian ink or diluted paint. This can be done using a brush. The children can hold the thread above a sheet of white paper and let the end of the thread stick to it. They pull the thread back gradually, or roll or wiggle it in several directions. Having done this several times, the children will discover that only thread can produce such interesting patterns and unique 'choreography'. The children might attempt to capture the fundamental lines on a separate sheet of paper.

10   11

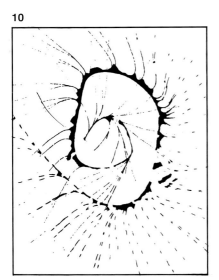

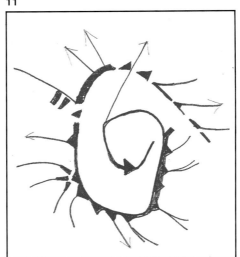

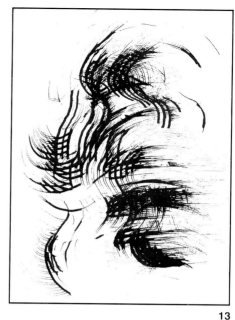

12

13

As demonstrated by rubbings, lines may have different shapes. They differ according to the tool we use when drawing. Children would discover far fewer of these shapes if we offered them merely a pen, a felt-tip or a pencil. Let us now try to discover how the lines are shaped when we use some objects charged with colour. For example, take a piece of thread. It reminds us of a line by its very shape but it will only come to life when children dip it in paint and learn to create marks on paper using various movements – wiggling, rolling,

12, 13, 14 *How to comb the dishevelled hair and curl it.* The children attempted to record these situations using a fragment of a comb whose teeth were pressed tightly to the paper surface. They noticed that it would hardly be possible to draw such a perfectly regular structure using any other tool. The multiplicity of lines seems to produce the optical illusion of movement. The children also tried other tasks, e.g., to capture the movement of a record in circles as opposed to the spiral tracing of a shell, and to sign themselves in 'multiples'.

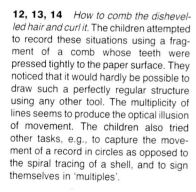

14

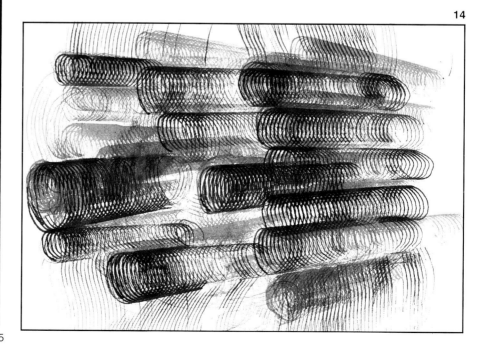

15

pulling it back gradually. We can even use slightly damp paper. As with rubbings, children can store their works for future creative activities.

Whatever tool we use when drawing, the line is always the result of some sharp point. A fragment of a comb, which we offer children to use in the following activities, has many teeth arranged regularly next to each other. If we imagine that a piece of thread performs a solo dance as a ballerina would, then the comb dipped in a shallow dish of paint will produce something completely different thanks to its numerous regular lines. Even though at this

15, 16, 17 *Clothes brush marks.* The children squeezed out 'stripes' of various shades of tempera paint directly onto a sheet of paper, and then moved a dry brush quickly across them. In further exercises, they carefully wetted the brush points in a shallow dish of Indian ink and tried to visualise some movements, such as brushing specks of dust off a coat. Some children attempted to suggest a bird's feather in flight. They used a longer goose feather.

16

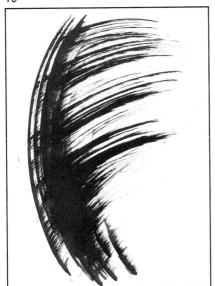

17

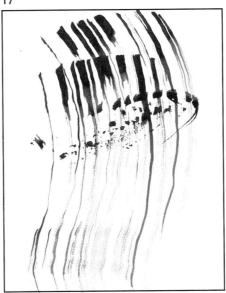

18, 19, 20 *Marks of sponge movements.* The surface of a sponge has an interesting structure. At first, the children dipped the sponge in a thicker paint and imprinted its whole surface on paper. Later, they only used its edge, so that the result was a structure of lines. The children were interested in observing the lines gradually fade and disappear. Before their work became truly creative, as shown in the illustrations, they had to practise various movements of the sponge on several sheets of paper. It is important to provide advice and help in order that the children, deeply involved in this activity, do not make their clothes and the whole place too dirty. The paints should be diluted and spread over a larger area, preferably a palette.

18

stage it is just play and discovering what can be created by the comb, let us ask children what a drawing produced by the comb reminds them of. The answers might be, for example, a dishevelled beard; tousled or combed hair; a bird's nest in a tree; the quiet flow of a stream or shooting rapids; rain in a puddle. Or perhaps it may remind them of the furrows in a ploughed field or a print-out of an electrocardiograph.

If we give children an old clothes brush they discover that it is also composed of sharper points which, in contrast to the comb, are arranged over a surface. What marks will it leave? The brush is better suited to the quicker

19 **20**

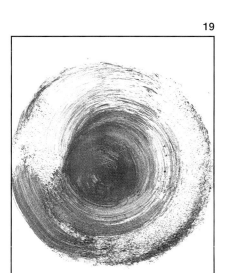

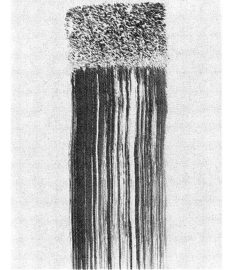

21

22

Marks made by a block of wood. There are several tasks which children were asked to perform. They involved the arrangement of thinner, thicker and 'gradually disappearing' lines over the entire area:

21 The intertwining and overlapping of groups of lines (similar to the manner in which mats are woven); also, the counterbalancing of varied directions over the entire area of a sheet of paper.

22 The regular order of lines is suddenly disturbed by a 'disorderly quarrel' of marks produced by the flat block of wood.

23 Twisted and spiral lines are not easily executed when using the flat block of wood. However, they are well worth the effort.

24 How do we weave a basket?

and lighter strokes (in order that colours do not mix) which children should practise before they start to draw. Let them begin by brushing specks of dust off their coats in several directions. Only afterwards should they attempt to draw on sheets of paper. Again the finished drawings may remind them of something, for instance the jet of a cascading fountain, the fur of a frightened cat, or the needles of a porcupine.

Children are undoubtedly familiar with a bathroom sponge – an object of fun

Children will soon discover what the flat block of wood is able to produce when differently turned. They can also be reminded that some experienced graphic artists use a flat pen or a flat brush to produce writing in which the horizontal lines are thin and the vertical lines are thick.

23

24

18

The tool determines the line produced. Let us remind ourselves that the shape of lines depends on the sensitive use of a tool. The line itself contributes to the highly individual nature of what is drawn. Before children draw a portrait, a tree, or anything else, they should first decide which tool to use. One kind of tool will be needed for the portrait of an angry grandfather and another for the drawing of a willow or a feather. Let us consult our sampler to see what the lines produced by various tools look like: pencil – pen – charcoal – brush – flat block of wood – felt-tip pen – several felt-tip pens bunched together – string rubbing – spray-gun with paint (for line casting and spraying line).

and games whose linear marks they can also record. The sponge can be thrown or dropped. The record of various movements of the sponge, whose edge has been dipped in paint and drawn lightly over a sheet of paper, can often remind us of the photograph of a fast-moving object.

Finally, when children have assembled and displayed all their drawings made with these unfamiliar tools, they will immediately realise how individual marks differ from one another.

So far thick and thin lines have been produced by unfamiliar tools. Now we can prepare for children a simple 'universal' tool which is capable of forming various lines. We cut out a small flat piece of wood and show children how to draw a variety of thick and fine lines. Children learn how to handle this tool with confidence and ease if we ask them to perform several simple tasks involving various types of lines.

A Slanted axe cuts have created an amazingly balanced structure across the parallel cracks of a chopping block. It is possible to draw or make a rubbing of this geometrically plastic 'construction'.

B Leaf filaments. Just as a spider's web is an engineer's network in space, leaf filaments are a network over a surface. Children might magnify it in their drawing.

C Čestmír Kafka (1922–1988) from the Cycle 'On Linking Two Objects', 1980–83, sewn collage, paper, 69.5 × 100.5 cm
When looking around with children we can notice many multi-purpose 'interfaces', i.e., links of smaller and bigger shapes composed of different materials which seem to be tied together. They are either 'in an agreement' and are united, or they are opposed to a 'mutual dialogue' by their shapes. In this Cycle (as in a diary), the artist records 'comic and serious tales linking two objects'. However, not only two objects are involved. We could take it further, metaphorically speaking, and refer to close or 'broken' links to friends, favourite books, and so on.

D Lee Ufan (b. 1936) 'From a Line', 1978, drawing on a canvas using a stone, 162 × 130 cm
This drawing includes an outstanding awareness of the medium used; a perfect method of creative expression; a masterly gesture involving deep concentration and thought by the artist. In a single line whose colour fades one might anticipate the fundamental principle of life – i.e., birth, the passage of time, death and decay.

E Zdeněk Sýkora (b. 1920) 'Line No. 26', 1984, oil on canvas, 150 × 150 cm
The author fed a programme to a computer which continued the colour and linear order of curves. The painter subsequently selected the most interesting part of infinite oscillation, as if viewed through binoculars, on a large canvas. This resembles records of stars and planets orbiting in infinite space.

20

C

D

E

26

Capturing a Mood in Your Drawing

Can we draw 'the invisible' – motion, sound, music? Can we capture in various lines our moods and emotions, a conversation or an argument between two people?

In Chapter One, when children were expressing verbally the differences between various lines, we noticed that very often they used comparisons. The lines might be either shy and quiet or courageous and fierce, as if the children could visualise different characteristics of people and different phenomena of the natural world. It is easier to record a motion than to visualise a sound or a mood. The motion passes in time but, nevertheless, it is visible. Take the work of an astronomer, a meteorologist or an air-traffic controller. These people all 'read' images of various movements, which they are able 'to visualise' in their records and graphs. In these images three fundamental characteristics of motion, i.e. direction, speed and shape in the form of curves and parallels, are linked and can be observed. It might be interesting for us to note how these three characteristics of motion can be expressed by differing features of lines. Let us imagine the sky as a screen – children will substitute a large sheet of paper for it. Children are not going to draw clouds, an aeroplane or a circling bird of prey as representing the landscape but they are

25 *When I am sad, I start singing.* This illustration was produced in two stages. Firstly, the children were asked to express a particular mood in colour. The particular mood being conveyed was sadness. In most cases the children used quick strokes of a sponge or a brush dipped in a colour corresponding to their particular mood. Later, they considered the change of mood. In this instance they considered how to relieve their feeling of sadness. Would meeting a friend, reading a book, or singing a song help? Here the child decided upon a cheerful song. It is expressed by a fine white line made with a thin brush.

26 *Wind and fire.* The children used the sharp lines of brush points dipped in red and black tempera in order to express the different characteristics and movements of these natural elements. They used an extra sheet of paper to cover the interfaces of the various shapes. The unfamiliar tools referred to in Chapter One could also be used. Expressing a movement, or a mood, which is transitory, calls for a fairly rapid recording, which might be done by using those tools. We might suggest other themes, such as: 'Water and fire', 'Wind and water', 'Thunderstorm and heavy rain' or 'Snowstorm'.

27

27 Feelings evoked by the arrangement of lines and shapes:
1 Horizontal parallels – peace, stillness
2 An oblique line and a meandering line – differentiation of various movements
3 Sharp upward lines – excitement
4 Symmetrical division – balance, agreement, understanding
5 Repetition of elements – emphasis, command, striking rhythm
6 Equal formations – harmony, balance
7 Contradiction of a 'soft' and 'hard' formation – conspicuous contradiction, contrast, disagreement
8 Various directions of lines – contradictory tensions (e.g., in motion)
9 Asymmetry – tension, disagreement

Children might attempt to match the captions with the illustrations in the following situations: 'Walking my dog', 'Getting on with my brother or sister', 'Today's important chores' (recommended illustrations 2, 4, 5).

going to record three different motions. Firstly, children create a delicate impression of gradually receding and slightly undulating parallels (to represent clouds). Secondly, they draw a thick straight line (to represent an aeroplane). Thirdly, they create thinner circular lines ending suddenly in a straight line (to represent a bird of prey). Children will experience and record the beauty of motion differently from the manner in which it is looked upon by an astronomer, a meteorologist or an air-traffic controller.

Lines recording different motions, sounds and moods can be differentiated

28   **29**

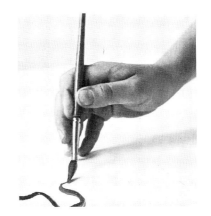

28, 29, 30, 31 *Movements of water.*
When diving and swimming in a swimming pool we can observe the wave patterns. When swimming in river we can observe the undulation of the waves, and the calmer or nearly smooth surface of the current. From a bridge we can see the interesting appearance and gradual disappearance of a ship's swell. We can produce different impressions of the water marks made by bathroom taps and showers. Even the ripples caused by throwing stones into water can provide us with suggestions. Can children recognise jumping into water, whirlpools and slow current in the illustrations? Can they guess where the illustrators used a quick stroke of a sponge or a thin brush, in contrast to using the technique of rubbing?

30

not only by shape but also by their arrangement over an area. When children have finished any of the drawings suggested in this chapter, they can compare them with the graphic table 27. This table illustrates various lay-outs of an area, which may help to explain why some drawings evoke feelings of peace and tranquillity while others evoke feelings of excitement or tension. However, this table is not the definitive model. After all, drawings are individual statements of children's feelings and concepts. Drawings reflect children's own experience. Children may have their own explanations for their creations, and these may not coincide with ours.

31

A lively line is created by applying or releasing pressure with a brush. It is important for children to dip a brush in paint or Indian ink in such a way that it makes the resulting line as steady and as long as possible. The tip of the brush will obviously create the most delicate lines.

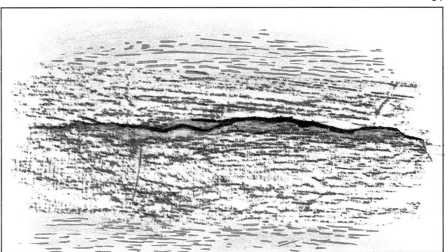

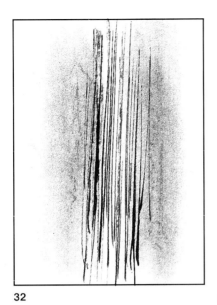

32

33

32, 33 *Quiet humming* and *Slamming the door* are the recordings of contrasting sounds produced by a pen and a comb. While the children were creating these lines they made comments on their work, such as: 'I was all alone at home, and it was very quiet. However, when I began to listen carefully, I realised that I had forgotten to switch off the record player. It was going round and round, humming quietly. Then I opened a window and, suddenly, BANG! The draught slammed the door but it did not close properly and began to squeak.'

Let us explain to children that in contrast to musical tones, sounds are created by irregular vibrations. In their drawings children can use either sounds which they have arranged to occur, or sounds which they have 'hunted' and recorded in the world of sounds. However, it is important to be able to listen to sounds and differentiate them into soft or loud sounds; sounds with oscillations; sounds of lengthy or momentary duration. By these means different drawings of household sounds (e.g. sewing machine, fridge, footsteps or bathroom sounds), or sounds in the street, in the park, in the railway station or in the zoo can be produced. Whether expressing the sounds in drawings while listening to them or recalling them later from memory children

34

35

34, 35 *Kittens' quietly purring and miaowing* made with a block of wood and *A little dog barking at an Alsatian* made with the edge of a ruler dipped in paint, are easily distinguishable. You can also 'read' in the recording that the Alsatian successfully scared away the little dog with a few barks. These sounds, which contrast in nature and noise level, are expressed by the lines.

36 *Scraping on a fiddle in the sitting room* was made by gradually pulling a string dipped in paint. It naturally does not reflect the marvellous tones which can be produced on a violin by somebody who is able to play it well. This unpleasant scraping on a fiddle hurts our ears!

36

should first decide which tool and colour tone they will use for individual sounds. For example, the forest does not have to murmur only 'in green'.

The tones of musical instruments come from regular vibrations of, for example, a string (our vocal cords vibrate when we sing). To listen with understanding to a violin concert or a choir performance is a real treat for the receptive listener. Naturally, he or she will concentrate fully on the beauty of the music itself and only later will be willing to render these tones into lines or colours. If we want to combine listening to music with a creative activity, we

37

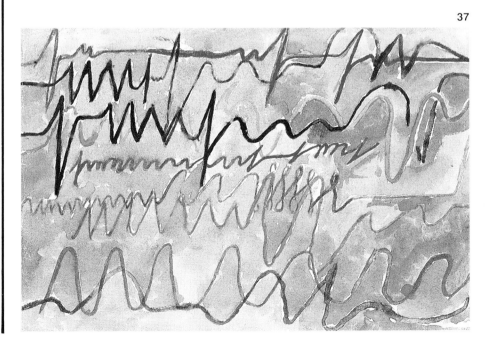

37 *Impressions of songs* in lines made by a thin brush or pastels on a colour background, captured the rise or fall of a melody; the maintenance or changes in the rhythm. The lines seem to convey a harmonious mood, expressing the pleasure we experience when we sing.

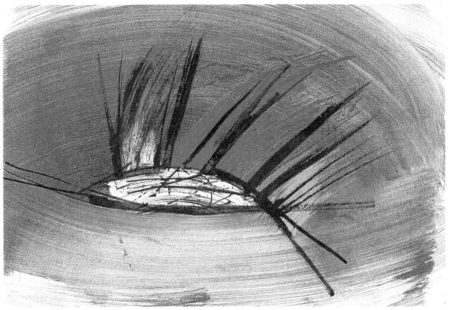

38

38 *Witnessing a car crash.* This experience was so strong that even its creative image is very convincing. Looking at it we might sense the collision, the noise of shattering glass, perhaps the moaning and cries for help. This exercise involved working over the surface of the paper with a sponge, followed by rapid strokes with a sharp brush.

can start by singing simple songs together – sad songs and happy songs – and reproduce in lines the rhythm of a melody, its rises and falls. We may also attempt to capture 'the colour mood' of a song. Later it is possible to select parts of musical compositions which contrast. For example, the creative expressions of the children who listened to parts of Debussy's *La Mer,* Honegger's *Pacific 231* and Prokofiev's *Peter and the Wolf* were rather striking.

From now on our creative tasks will be more complex as our drawings will be concerned with personal experience. Throughout our lives we experience

39

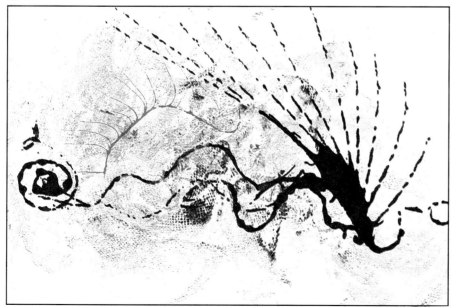

39 *How Mum scolded me.* Explanatory notes are written on the back of the illustration: 'Mummy was very upset because I had told a lie. She threatened to tell everything to Dad. I was very unhappy, so I curled up on a sofa in the sitting room and fell asleep.' Notice the widespread use of the line made with a string dipped in colour. Does the 'wiggling' of the lines remind you of being frightened of a smacking?

40 *I am rather puzzled.* This is a more complex impression by a twelve-year-old boy. He also used lines made with a string on surfaces coloured by the quick movements of a sponge. He explains his image in the following terms: 'I am not very good at maths. I feel rather puzzled by the maths, which is shown by those white lines. The red line represents an idea leading to the solution of a problem.'

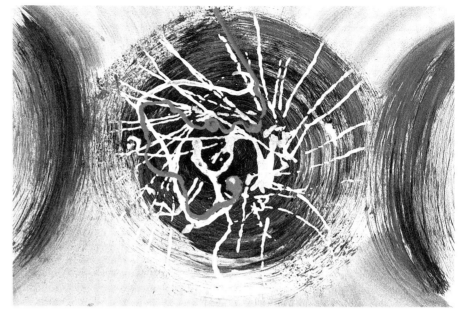

40

situations which evoke varied emotions – happiness, sadness, fear or hope. As children respond to many events emotionally rather than rationally they are likely to accept our suggestions without inhibitions. We might suggest that they express their feelings at winning a competition or a race in a drawing. Or we might ask them to express their feelings when they were apprehensive about a visit to the dentist, particularly if it was a miserable wet day! There are many situations when children experience great happiness or fear. We can also use some of the creative activities outlined in Chapter One (e.g. rubbing, lines drawn with thread) as a stimulus and inspiration for drawing.

41 *Crossing the street with my brother.* A younger boy explains his image of this experience: 'I collect my little brother from the nursery school in the afternoon. He is rather frightened to cross the busy street with me. I can never make up my mind when and where to cross. Once my brother ran ahead of me! So, when I finally manage to take him to the other side of the street I feel very relieved.' This boy showed great creativity by using the rubbing of his anorak's zip to convey the traffic in the street. In another variant the same boy used a toy car's wheels dipped in paint. Finally, he used a felt-tip pen to draw his troubles when crossing the busy street.

41

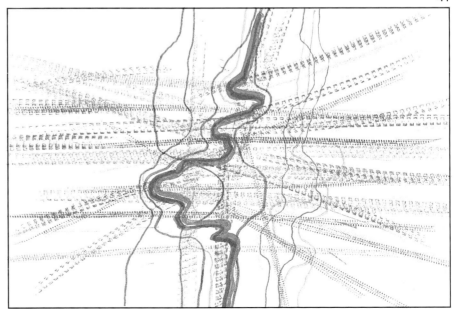

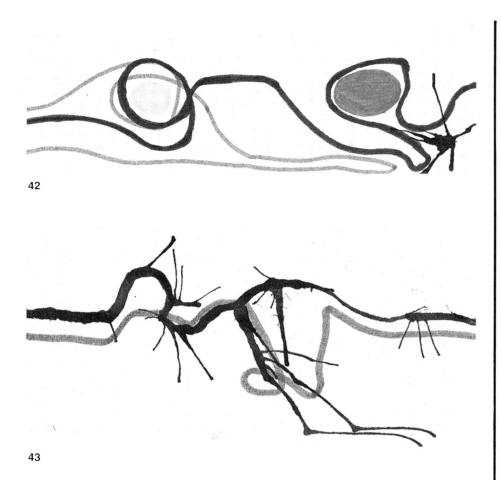

42

42 *Do not leave me, come back – we had a good time together.* A girl wrote this under her picture and added the explanation: 'My friend came to spend her holiday with me, but then she had to leave suddenly. We got on very well together. I used the black line to draw myself.' Children can try to recognise how these feelings of mutual understanding and sadness, which spring from loneliness, are expressed.

43

43 *Quarrelling with my older sister.* This illustration, which uses two lines, is explained by a younger brother: 'It always makes me very cross if my sister treats me like a small child. I shout at her and often start a fight with her. However, she always manages to calm me down, and even persuades me that she is in the right.' Children can guess which line the boy used to express his sister's behaviour.

By using lines we can tell stories. Is it also possible for lines 'to hold a conversation' with one another as people do? Let us attempt it with the children. Our discussion could start like this: 'How do you get along with your friend while you are playing? Has it ever happened that you two could not agree? Do you start an argument or is your friend the one who starts arguing? Do you think that your friend's ideas are sensible and go along with them? Or

44

44 *When two people have an argument.* A boy added a note to his picture: 'People hurt each other in an argument. The weaker one starts to cry as if something was hurting him. That round line is somehow shaken by the attacks of the sharp, jagged line.'

Children drew the pictures 42, 43, 44 using a brush, a felt-tip pen and a block of wood dipped in Indian ink. They also spread the drops of Indian ink by blowing at the surface while it was still wet.

45 *When we could not come to an agreement.* The children recorded a lively exchange of views in the class, using the multiple lines of a comb. The class members were unable to agree where to go for a school trip. The girls, represented later by the red lines, were more united than the boys. The boys, represented by the black lines, came up with different ideas. It is apparent that lines can even express the nature of discussions involving several participants!

45

do you find the ideas strange and not like them? You must have spoken to somebody this afternoon. How did your talk go? Try to express it using two lines. The first line will show your impression of your friend's talk and the second line will show what *you* said. If there were three of you, add one more line. A weaker softer line seems to calm things down, to give in, or it perhaps shows fear and flight. A stronger firmer line is evidence of a leader, one who lends support. Another line may express anger, quarrelling or bullying.'

A *A stone with treble linear structures.* Children deciphered the stone's surface as 'father's talk' (represented by strong plastic lines), 'mother's talk' (represented by heavy black cracks), and 'children's talk' (represented by minute and very restless lines).

B Karel Malich (b. 1924)
'Countryside with Eternity', 1980–83, sculpture from wire, bronze netting, colours and threads, 250 × 124 × 239 cm
A sculptor's narrative about time and motion in space seems to have no end. The lines forever circle in oval curves, as if they were stars orbiting in space or electrons colliding in an atom. In a landscape of curves there are primordial cells in earth-brown colour, and life's reds and yellows. These represent the artist's impression of eternity.

C Jaromír Rybák (b. 1952)
'Blue Cloud', 1988, glass sculpture, 39 × 21 × 12 cm
It seems that all the motions of various forms of water are enchanted in a transparent icy obelisk. Water whirls like a cloud of steam; it drops down in a shower of rain or snow. Water droplets wish to return from the depths of the Earth back to their original clouds.

D Karel Malich (b. 1924)
from the Cycle 'Light', 1987, pastel, 102 × 73 cm
The children discussed this painter's portrayal of the eye, which captured the movement of a sun's ray, and analysed it as the spectrum of a rainbow. One realises in this divided code, set against the retina of the eye where its 'intelligent' cells are situated, just what he, in fact, observes. The picture might, perhaps, represent light messages and the eye's 'thoughts'.

E *Barley heads.* They seem to be involved in a sort of a 'dialogue'. Can the children try to guess which voice is more eloquent and more emphatic in contrast to the voice which is more patient, and even employs constructive arguments in its reasoning?

F *Agates* talk about themselves; about the secret of their birth; about immense hydro-thermal processes in the Earth's depths; about the infinite passage of geological time. The outer zones of an agate are the oldest – the stone grew from its edge towards its centre.

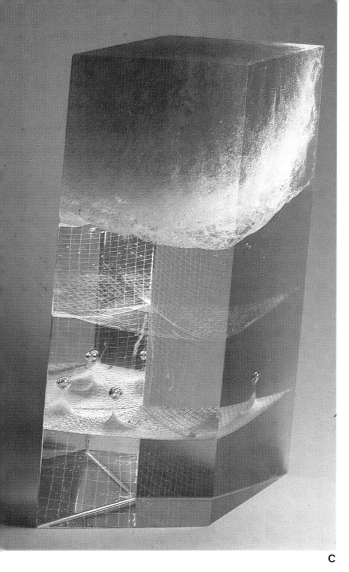

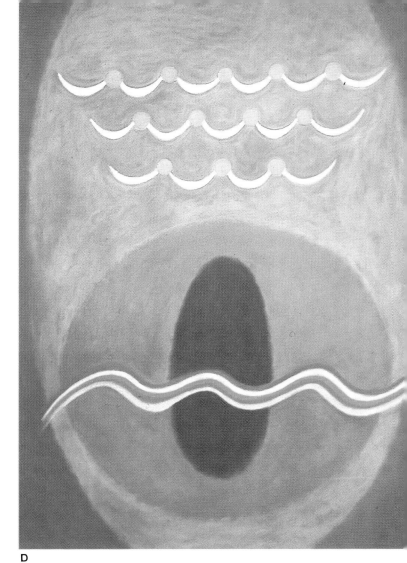

C

D

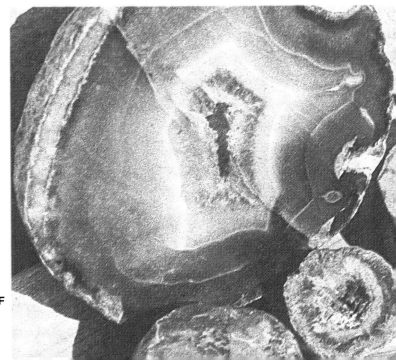

E F

46

3

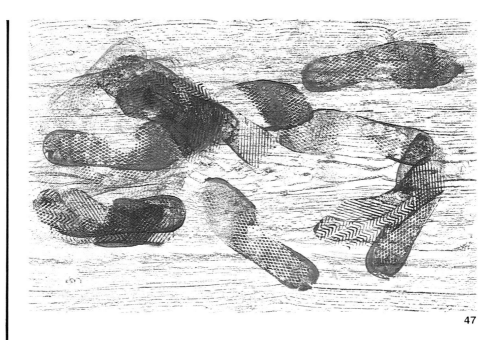

47

Human Footprints

What do our footprints reveal about us? What do angry stampings look like? What marks do we leave when tiptoeing? 'Foot graphics'. In praise of our shoes.

---

46 *Thoughtless Mr Trampler,* who apparently misbehaves in the forest, is created by gluing together the sole prints produced in various activities by human footprints. The children completed the background in Indian ink and colour pastels.

47 *The record of a dance* was made using paint-covered soles. The children laid a large piece of paper on the floor. Next to it they put plastic boards on which coloured paints were spread. The children also prepared clean shoes to change into. They switched on their favourite music and rehearsed their 'performance'. They then stepped on the paint-covered boards and danced on the paper in their paint-covered soles.

The portrait which is a creative statement about a person is not only an accurate record of the human face. It is also an attempt to understand an individual's psyche: what he thinks, what he touches, where his steps – even those seemingly in vain – take him. Footsteps have contributed greatly to the history of the world. Sir Edmund Hillary, the famous New Zealand mountaineer, took his first step in life as a toddler; he then took hundreds of thousands of steps to school; and then many other steps, including the very step which took him, as the first human, to the summit of Mt. Everest – the highest mountain in the world. Obviously, we all take steps and it would be a great pity if they led us nowhere. It is worth noting these steps, in order to visualise them and learn from them. Although our awareness how we walk is subconscious, much is revealed by our steps – our mood, our immediate state of mind, and such qualities as decisiveness, hesitancy, impatience, fear, alertness or weariness. A walking style completes the psychical and physical portrait of an individual. The footprint – this 'visualisation' which occurs

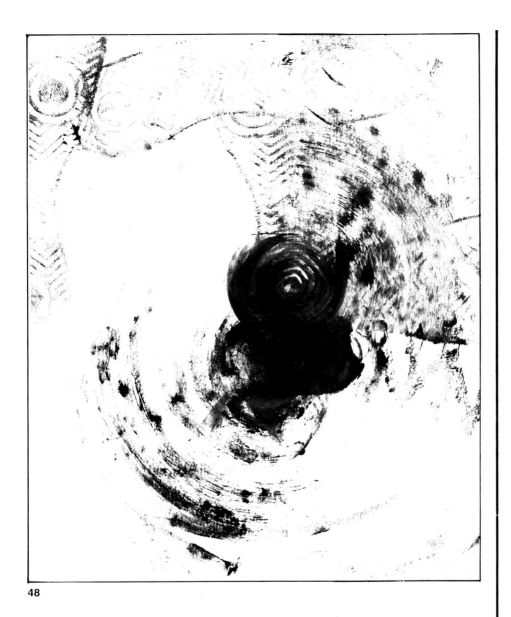

48

If the children cannot make these impressions outside, we then prepare inside a large sheet of plastic with two large sheets of paper. One piece of paper will be used for making the footprints. The other piece will be used for changing into clean shoes (we place these next to the paper). We then spread a layer of tempera on a large plastic board using a wide brush or a roller. We also have to clean the soles of those shoes which are to be used for 'footprint graphics'. (Immediately after finishing such creative activities we have to wash these shoes again.) Once the children have rehearsed their 'performance', they can put on their 'working' shoes, step on to the painted board and then onto the paper.

between the sole and the ground – will, therefore, form the basic of 'footprint graphics'. The sole of our shoe will become an unusual tool.

The way in which children use it is easily discovered from the accompanying picture and caption. At first we try to visualise simple situations and create a footprint folio. What print do we leave when we shuffle impatiently from one foot to another on the spot? What prints do we make when we slip; when we stand on tiptoe; or when hanging out the washing? Children should rehearse their 'performance' before they step on paper in paint-covered soles. Otherwise quite often they halt suddenly or move hesitantly and the impression is far from convincing. It might be useful for them to accompany their graphic performance verbally, for example: 'Brrr-brr, how cold it is!' (jumping up and down on the spot), 'Shhhh, I mustn't wake up Granny!'

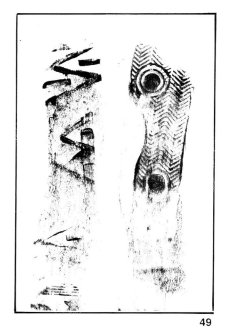

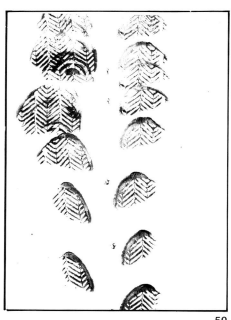

49

50

(tiptoeing), 'Ouch, ouch, it's my sprained ankle again!' (limping). Children soon discover other possibilities. What about stamping a foot to scare away a dog? Or jumping for joy? Completed 'drawings' can be interpreted later to see which mood or emotion the 'footprint graphics' captured.

Older children could try simple situations in which there are several participants using larger sheets of paper. These could include impressions of meetings or even dancing.

51

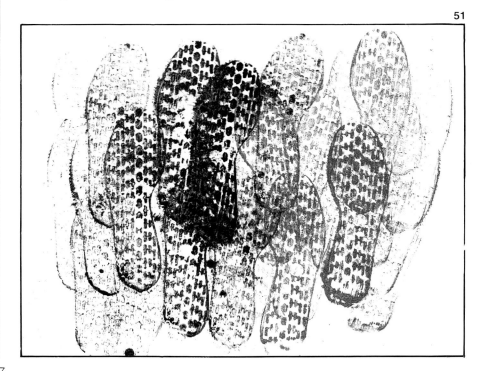

50, 51 *The recording of tiptoeing* and *The recording of anger.* Both the footprints created and the situations depicted are in direct contrast. Can the children explain these impressions?

52

52 *A paper swallow's sad end.* This work looks more like a poster. Somebody has spitefully trampled on a paper toy. In this instance the footprints are vicious and have symbolic meaning. Children suggested other themes for 'bad shoes', which by their ruthlessness destroy Nature, or the work and pleasure of others.

'Footprint graphics' were made by children placing their hands in the shoes.

There are further senses in which we can observe human footprints. For example, let us note various sayings related to 'our way of life' and 'the ways of human behaviour'. Along this 'way' we often stumble, avoid obstacles, get out of step or even step out. Every culture has sayings of which children are aware, and which they can adapt and illustrate. For example: 'He is so clumsy, he acted like a bull in a china shop', and 'Only a wicked person would stamp on a child's toy'.

Younger children, who are more likely to use realism in their understanding of footprints, can also try 'footprint graphics' with a more concrete content. The most important point is to be able to see something interesting in the

53 *My mistake*. A boy explains his illustration in these terms: 'I took a wrong step; I stepped out of line; I made a mistake and now I am very sorry.' The red footprints represent an unpleasant mistake.

54 *I am impatient*, 'I'd rather run away. It feels as if I were walking on a hot pavement or tarmac . . .' The illustration is based on these initial ideas. The red footprints seem to be turning impatiently as if seeking an escape from those hot surfaces.

53

impression of a patterned sole. It is a good idea to move the marks of footprints around. We can complete them by imprinting the shoe-tip with our hand in the shoe. At other times it might be enough to shade footprints in Indian ink. If a cluster of footprints reminds the children of something they can cut it out. Then they can glue it onto another sheet of paper and complete the effect in ink or colour (see the introductory picture *Mr Trampler*). The illustration on page 41 may also suggest a way of doing it.

If children did not want to make a print of the whole sole they covered over some pieces of the paper using an extra sheet.

54

55

55 *Galloping horses.* These appeared when one impression of a slide was completed by drawing. A boy became interested in the pattern of a sole with smaller and bigger circles which reminded him of the horse's eyes and nostrils. He only added the mane and the ears.

Children are avid collectors. They might be interested in collecting various shoe-sole designs. If they decide to do this they could try the technique of colouring soles with water-based paint rather than the technique of rubbing.

It is only right that we sing the praises of our shoes, as without them we would not get far. People invented shoes for comfort as Nature had omitted to take our comfort into consideration. Let us, therefore, ask the children to make a drawing of a life-size shoe. They might be interested in drawing a sports

56

56 *Pussy Quiet-Paws* can walk as quietly as if she moved on cushions. This illustration is a fine example of the sensitive handling of a shoe with a fine sole pattern. The children placed their hands in the shoe. In front of them was a large sheet of paper and a board covered with well-diluted black paint. The children used only a part of the sole to make impressions.

57 *Fish.* Children suddenly discovered the shape of a fish in a cluster of footprints on the paper used in the previous creative activities. They cut out the 'caught' fish and glued it onto another piece of paper. It was a simple task to complete the details of the fish's body and the background. It is apparent that this fish, with richly coloured fins, represents the sort of fish seen in an aquarium. The children's version was enlarged.

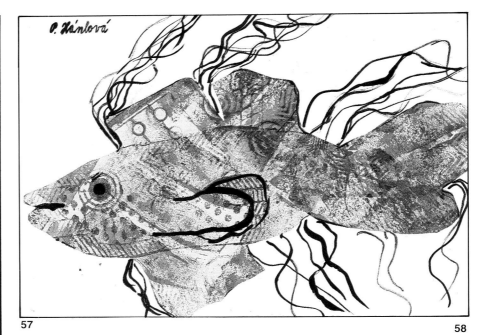

57

58

58 *The Sultan's portrait* was created in a similar fashion to 'Pussy Quiet-Paws'. However, it is not very easy to decide which part of the sole might provide you with the very shape needed. In order to make sure that you imprint what you really want, you should gradually cover the already completed parts of your picture with an extra sheet of paper.

41

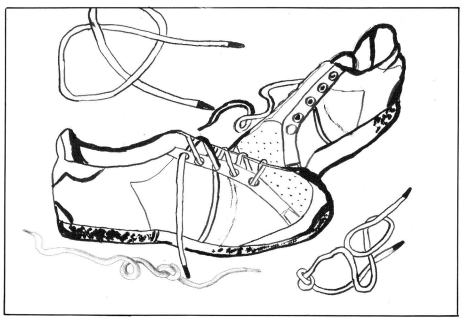

59

59 *My favourite shoes*. This drawing from a model is well situated on the surface. Can the children distinguish the right shoe from the left shoe? It is rather difficult to draw this properly. It might be helpful to draw the shoe true to scale, which makes it easier to check its fundamental shape and proportions. The children might like to emphasise the most important features of the shoe with lines (e.g., its shape and its individual parts).

shoe, which is suitable as a model both for shape and texture. They might use hiking boots or studded football boots; skiing or skating boots. Some might prefer high-heeled shoes or summer sandals as models for drawing. Children could also try to design sports or summer shoes for themselves.

60 **a**

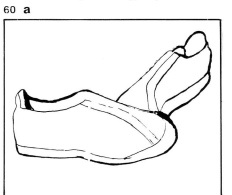

b

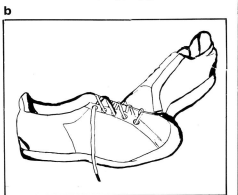

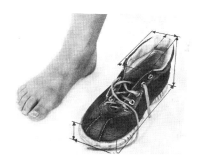

c

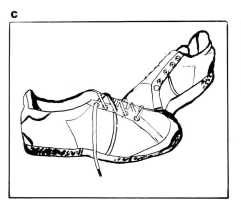

d

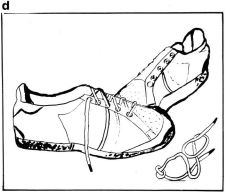

60 Note the individual stages of the drawing. The children first pencilled the axis and fundamental proportions of the shoe – its length, height, and breadth. They then drew the shoe itself in vivid lines (a). They observed the same procedure when drawing the second shoe (b). They gradually added further surface divisions (c). Finally, they drew in the detail – e.g., eye holes, laces.

61, 62, 63 *Magical shoes.* The children used their imagination in order to complete the shoe as a means of transport. At first they only added the cut-out 'technical parts' to the drawing of a shoe. They did not glue these parts onto the paper because they were able to play with them, and vary them. Children might also find it interesting to complete their real old shoe with various small objects. These additional devices enable the wearer to walk on an air cushion and on thin ice. They also enable the wearer to fly. Hermes, in his role as messenger to the Gods, must have worn similar shoes. Nowadays any postman would be thrilled at the prospect of having such a useful pair of shoes!

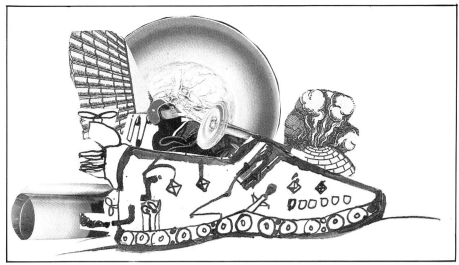

61

Projecting 'the shadow' of a shoe on a sheet of paper with the help of a bedside lamp might help us to produce the basic outline of a shoe.

In legends and fairy tales shoes are endowed with magic qualities. Shoes help their wearers to fly in the air or to take seven-league steps.

In our illustrations you can see numerous examples of 'fairy tale' shoes. Children can make use of previous drawings or they can cut out a picture of a bigger shoe from a mail order catalogue. They might glue the picture onto a sheet of paper and, using their imagination, draw in 'additional' devices – e.g., folding wings, a propeller, or a rocket engine in the heel of the shoe. This technique, which uses magazine and newspaper cuttings glued to the pictorial surface, is known as 'collage'.

62

63

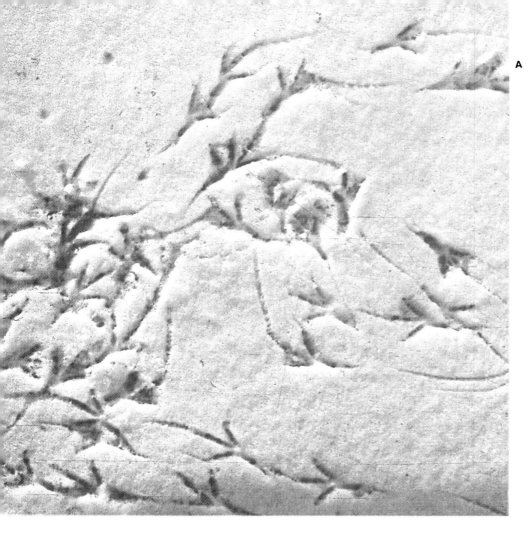

A

B

A *Birds' footprints* in a dusting of snow are a fragile record of an action; of birds arguing, leaping forward and turning back, searching for a destination. How clumsy the prints of people hurrying to their cosy homes seem in contrast to the tiny prints of the birds' world, living 'shoe-less' throughout the long winter. It is as if they wrote down their experience on a 'sheet of white paper', and sent us this letter written in a secret code which can be read from several angles. It is rather difficult to guess how many tiny 'writers' have contributed to this letter.

B *A ploughed furrow* on an immaculate snow surface bears witness to how difficult it might have been to make people's paths. At first only one pair of legs tries to check out the suitability of the terrain. If they are successful their prints are trodden by other people. However, they do not tread on the very first footprints but are satisfied to follow in their direction only. Those who are the last to follow find the path without furrows, as it is nicely trodden and easily traversed.

C Tomáš Ruller (b. 1957)
'Works Primarily Drawn', 23 December 1987, presentation
If the children attempted making footprints or hand prints on a sheet of paper, they unintentionally came close to so-called body-art. The author, a sculptor, presented in his performance a strong impression for himself and his audience, too. Through his own physical effort he gradually became a 'painter's revelation' in a ritual through which he verified himself as a mark – an imprint of coloured matter. Body-art has more forms, and also more representations, in world culture.

D Jiří Sozanský (b. 1946)
from the Cycle 'Incident' (detail), 1981–87, 240 × 180 cm
The picture called 'The Sad End of a Swallow' in this chapter is, in fact, the creative record of an endeavour calling attention to the fact that not all people are good. This artist's painting does not claim anything specific. Indeed, life's struggle – a tragedy – is depicted in black and red tangles, in apparently moving prints of human bodies.

C

D

4

65

Human Hands

Drawing the palm and fingers of a hand. 'Shadow theatre'. Can you communicate by gestures? Drawings of hand activity. Hands in the history of mankind.

64 *What can human hands do?* Architects' and builders' hands can build a town; fruit-growers' hands can transform a plot of land into an orchard; human hands can protect Nature. Can the children recognise whose hands are depicted in this illustration? It was made by two children who used the technique of rubbing and then completed their work in collage. We will speak about similar works towards the end of this chapter.

65 *That is the Earth, that is not the Sun,* since it has human hands instead of rays. Children made impressions round the 'head' with their wet hands. They then traced these impressions in Indian ink. In the coloured background a sunny day alternates with night. This looks more like a poster.

The creative interpretation of the hand in a drawing often expresses the mental well-being of the person depicted. The hand is symbolic of numerous human activities and inventiveness. However, it is also symbolic of destructive forces. In our introductory talk the children should come to an understanding of why human hands are the focus of creative activities. Let us imagine that we have no hands, by putting them in our pockets. Almost immediately we have to ask somebody to open the door for us, to pour us a drink or tie our shoelaces. When we consider the hand we soon discover what makes it truly wonderful. It is our thumb! Note how cleverly it is placed in relation to the other fingers. We can demonstrate how indispensable the thumb really is in an easy experiment. We tape the thumb to the palm of our hand and attempt to button up a shirt. See, how we suddenly become clumsy! Whatever human beings want to do or invent is entrusted to the hands. The hands are also our most accessible models for creative activities, and are thus well worth close examination.

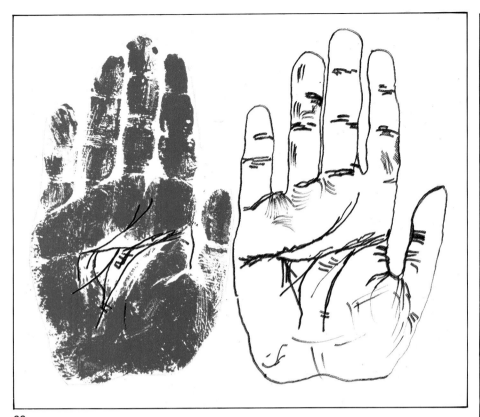

66

66 *The impression and the drawing of a hand.* The children first spread a thick paint on a plastic board, using a rubber roller in order to get a uniformly thick layer of paint. (A similar roller is used by graphic artists and photographers). The children placed their left hand into the paint and made several impressions on the paper. Using a block of wood dipped in Indian ink they emphasised the 'wrinkles' on the palms of their hands and their finger divisions. They then drew the hand independently in Indian ink, next to the impressions of their hands.

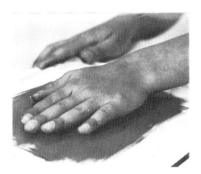

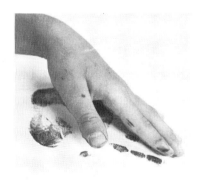

Firstly, let the children have a look at the left hand – its lines, its proportions and fingers. The burden of mental or physical work and daily worries create not only characteristic features in the face but also help to form the shape of the hand. It is interesting to note that a broad face corresponds to short broad hands, while a narrow face corresponds to long narrow hands. There is also the more rare so-called 'psychic' hand which is medium-size, with slim fingers and subtle lines on the palm. Children like to compare their soft small hands with the hands of their parents. It is similarly interesting to observe the minute papillary lines on the fingertips using a magnifying glass. These lines stay unchanged during our lifetime and no two people in the world have identical markings. The thumbmark is said to be far more individual than a person's signature. This phenomenon has been examined in China for hundreds of years. It has been calculated that there are sixty-four billion different combinations of fingerprints. In the last century, Sir Francis Galton, the famous English forensic scientist, divided the markings of fingerprints into four fundamental types (picture 68). Non-recurrent differences are based on the numbers and linking of the tiniest lines. Children can verify Galton's discovery by comparing the left thumb prints of their friends' hands.

Hands become the first toys for small babies. Many games for toddlers have been devised using the palm and fingers, often accompanied by nursery rhymes. The palm can become a shallow dish; hands can be piled on top of

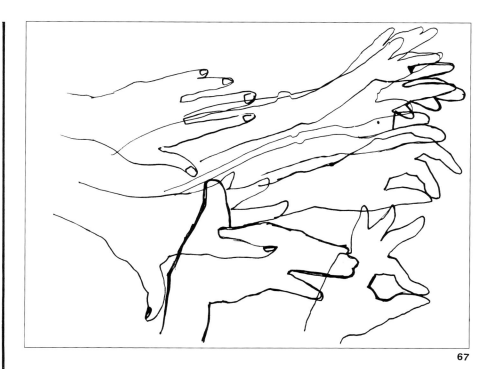

67

67 *The shadow theatre of the hands.*
The children preferred to draw the shadow outlines of the hand in felt-tip pen.
They attempted to achieve a greater
variety by drawing further stages of the
'shadow puppet's' movements in colour.
A friend's hand might be the model for
a drawing, provided he or she is patient.
The children can take turns in drawing
and 'shadow play'. They can practise
when the shadow of the hand becomes
larger or smaller. The size of the shadow
and its sharpness is in direct proportion to
the distance between the hand and the
bedside lamp.

68 *Mysterious lines on my thumb.* The
markings of fingerprints can be divided
into four basic types: the bow-like, the
loop left, the loop right and the spiral. The
children first imprinted their thumbs several times on the edge of the paper. They
then started their drawing from the centre
into the obvious directions of the bow,
loops or spiral. They used a magnifying
glass, and did not hesitate to enlarge their
drawings.

69 *The hand as an animated puppet.*
Younger children used a hand directly as
a template. They put it on the paper and
traced round it. They used their fingers
and various parts of the hand in order to
make other parts of the 'puppet's' body.
The children 'dressed' the puppet in a
colourful plaiting of tiny loops, which they
drew with felt-tip pens. They wanted it to
look like a funny glove.

each other; fingers can be 'woven' into a basket; fingers can become 'little
actors'. A fairy tale can be told and illustrated by hands forming shapes
between a bedside lamp and a white wall. These shadows suggest the
moving shapes of a dog, a goose, a cat or a bird. Our illustration shows how
simple it is to draw a rough outline – i.e., trace it on a sheet of paper using a felt-
tip pen. This is, in fact, another recognition of the structure and proportions of

68   **69**

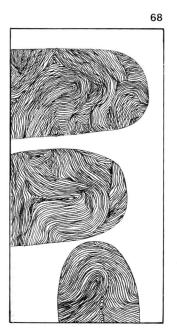

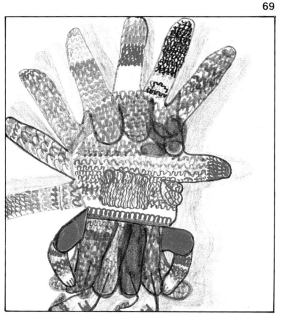

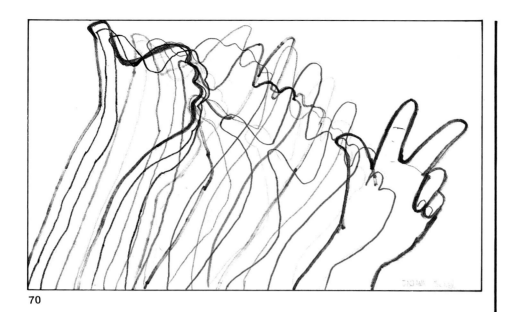

70

the hands, foreshortened in space. Children may try to draw where the thumb and the other fingers are concealed by the surface shadow. Younger children enjoy playing with the drawing of a shadow puppet (picture 69).

Can the hands talk? Let us record in writing what is conveyed by certain gestures. For example, knocking at the door – 'May I come in?', the finger placed at the mouth – 'Be quiet!', the raised index finger – 'Pay attention!', shaking hands – 'Welcome!'. Children can provide other examples, as there are a surprisingly large number of gestures to choose from. In our illustrations you will find many suggestions.

We then try to copy film animators. They have to draw numerous pictures in gradual stages. These pictures, when projected, give the illusion of actual movement. Our examples provide more information *(How I Count to Three; How I Throw a Ball)*.

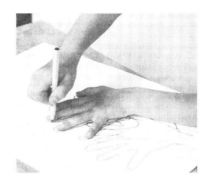

71

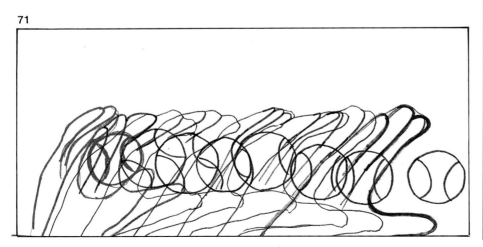

72 *How I picked up nails from the table.*
This illustration also records a gesture.
First the children practised the gesture in
two different ways. They then dipped the
hand in paint and expressed the gestures
in colour on a sheet of paper. Finally, they
drew the hand true to scale.

72

We can demonstrate simple activities directly on a piece of paper using
colour gestures. First, for example, we practise 'How I picked up nails from the
table', or 'How I first knocked at the door and then banged at it', or 'How to play
the piano (guitar or a drum)'. Second, that part of the hand which is used in the
movement over the surface is dipped in paint. We repeat the gesture – this

73

73 *Jolly hands.* Children drew a jolly
maze of their own hands. They traced
round their hands and completed them by
colour additions, depending on whose
hands they were. These could be the
hands of a musician playing colourful
notes; the hands of a girl stringing beads;
or the hands of a boy playing marbles.
What would the hands of a magician or
a gardener look like?

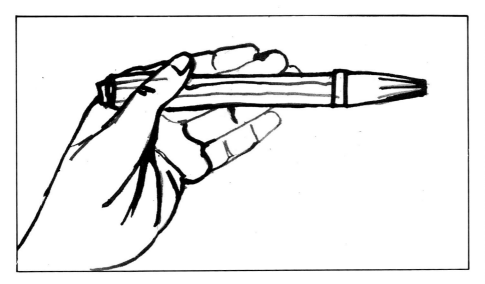

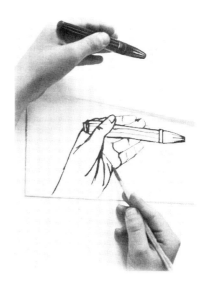

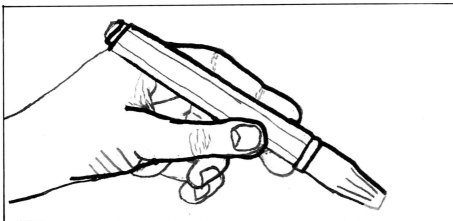

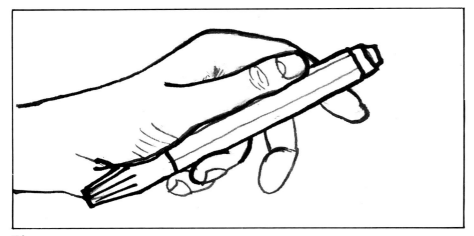

74

74 *How the hand changes when holding an object.* The object – in this instance the thick column of a felt-tip pen – provides a natural scale for drawing the proportions of the hand properly, and the correct position of the fingers. The children practised how the object could be held in three possible ways, and then traced its outline directly onto a sheet of paper three times. In Indian ink they then began to draw the hand true to scale from a model, holding the object in different ways.

▶

As a suggestion we would like to remind you of some objects which children could use in order to find out how the hand changes when holding different objects. Using a bedside lamp children could project the hand holding an object, as a shadow onto paper or a wall. This might be of some help in making the next drawing.

75 *How to hold the object in both hands.* The children used the technique of collage. They cut out a suitable object from a magazine. They also cut out hands which they had drawn previously. They put the hands and the object together.

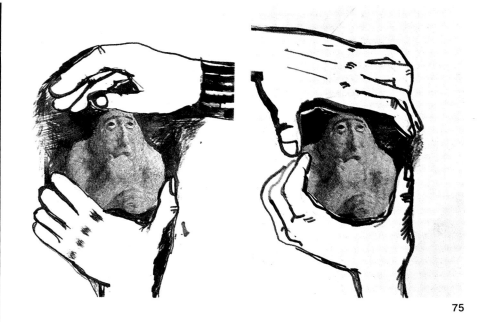

75

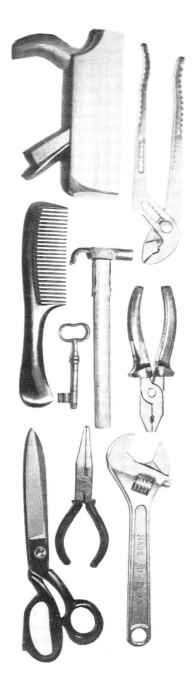

hand activity – in colour onto a sheet of paper. Finally, we draw the hand in a characteristic position a few times.

Let us remind the children that in prehistoric times the human hand evolved from activities performed by primitive man (e.g., grasping a branch or picking up a stone). We know the names of many inventors, however, at present we do not know when the first hominid began to bang two stones together, thus producing the first tool. We also do not know when the first 'upright' man *(Homo erectus),* three million years later, made a stone wedge with a blade and a blunt end which fitted the hand. This 'invention' is still taken into account by tool makers who heed the requirements of individual human activities. A surgeon holds his scalpel differently to the way a dressmaker holds her scissors. This unity of hand and object is our starting point, too. At first the children should draw, in pencil, a simple object, true to scale. They can trace its outline lightly on a sheet of paper. The shape of an object determines the proportions of our hand and the correct position of the fingers when holding the object. If, however, we find a magazine which shows a suitable object in a corresponding size to the depicted hand we can cut it out. Then we position our hands in a similar fashion to the shape of the object on a sheet of paper and practise how the object could be held in different ways. We roughly draw the fundamental positions of our hands by a vertically held pencil. These positions will serve as the starting point for drawing in Indian ink. Notice the illustration in which the children cut out the finished types of hand drawings and put them together with the object on a new sheet of paper (picture 75).

In the introductory part of this chapter we noted that the marks of the human hand were evident everywhere. Let us, therefore, illustrate what human hands are able to do. We show our admiration and respect by enlarging the human

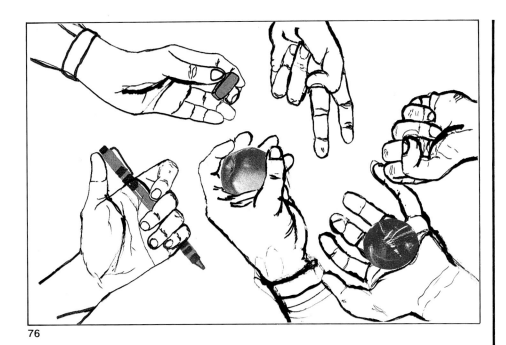

76

hands in the centre of a picture of the World. We use the techniques of rubbing, with a rolling pin, and collage, in which we make use of cut-outs of various human activities. If we collect pictures of houses, it might lead to a project called 'What the architects' hands can do'. However, there are many other projects which might be suggested, e.g., inventors' hands . . . glass makers' . . . dressmakers' . . . fishermen's . . . sportsmen's . . . mountaineers' . . . doctors' hands. The individual stages are illustrated in pictures 76, 77 and 78.

The children placed their hand on a sheet of firm paper and traced its outline. They cut out this shape. They ended up with 'two hands'. One hand was the cut-out, the other was there as a hole in the paper, and could also be used. They created an interesting composition out of these hands (it is possible to make use of several cut-out hands). The children placed softer paper on top of the composition. Next to it they placed an even surface (preferably glass) on which they spread a diluted oil-based paint or printers' ink, using a roller. They moved the roller over the thin paper, paying close attention to the fact that the paper should not move. The first part of their work was completed by this rubbing of the paper matrix. From magazines the children then cut out any pictures which would enable them to express what the hands can do. They glued these pictures in the empty spaces, and finally traced the hands in Indian ink or felt-tip pens.

77

78

77, 78 *What a conjuror's hands can do* and *Mother preserving fruit.*
These pictures were made using a technique combining rubbing and collage, and then completed by drawing. The accompanying photographs illustrate the procedure.

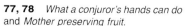

A Kurt Gebauer (b. 1941)
'Swimmers', 1969–74, textile and fibre glass, 50 × 150 cm
The most important movements for a swimmer are leg and arm movements. Even in this picture the figures are left hanging in space – an unusual situation. Children thought that the artist had 'sewn' his textile figures to resemble paleolithic Venuses. The figures are said to be 'fruit' on 'The Tree of Life'. Some children did appreciate the unique opportunity for matrons to float like ethereal beings. This enabled the children to imagine an unconventional human figure characterised by shape and movement. The facial features were not considered. K. Gebauer, as a polymath and with the eye of a sculptor, might remind us of César, whom he met in person in 1972. He is also a much sought-after designer of children's playgrounds.

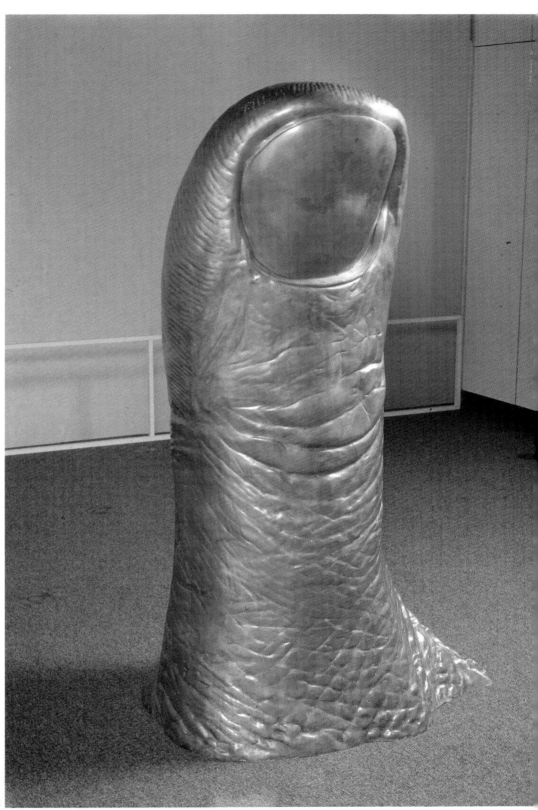

B César (César Baldaccini; b. 1921)
'Thumb', bronze sculpture
Albrecht Dürer (1471–1528) through his drawings, and August Rodin (1840–1917) through his sculptures, represent good examples of men who were interested in the human hand as an obvious sculptural form revealing an individual's characteristics and moods. César's *Thumb* is an anatomic statue which commemorates and celebrates the most dexterous and essential finger – the one which enables us to work. The thumb can also 'speak' through gesture – Gaius Julius Caesar, and other Roman Emperors, granted life or death to gladiators by a simple thumb movement.

B

5

80

Human Faces

Profile shadow plays. Playing with photographs. Distorting mirrors. Light and shade in the face. Personality as revealed in the face. What would your favourite uncle look like?

---

79 *A gallery of grandfathers.* The children used photographs to make their drawings. They realised that the wrinkled face of an older person is more distinctive, and thus easier to draw. They were asked to take the human face shown in a photograph and draw its corresponding linear structure, representing the type of hair or beard. In some instances the children wrote on the back of their illustrations what grandfather might be thinking about (e.g., 'I am strict but I would never smack you!'). These comments were based on the expression shown in the face.

80 *Albert Einstein's portrait.* A young boy, the author of this illustration, successfully interpreted characteristic features of the face of this eminent physicist (the shape of his hair and his wrinkles) from a photograph. This was done with vivid lines.

The first portrait which children might attempt is one of their mother. We note how similar 'mothers' look in these drawings. Children gradually come to identify characteristic features of the closest members of their family. Father is given a pair of glasses, Grandfather's face would not be complete without a beard and wrinkles. In the next stage of children's portrait drawing we observe that some children do not proceed beyond the stage of diagrams – a human head may look to us like that of a snowman or familiar faces seen in cartoons. This is a great pity, as there is nothing so remarkable as human faces. They reflect not only age but also moods and personalities. The child 'reads' the human face from the earliest stages of life. So let the children attempt a thorough 'reading' of the human face with a pen or a pencil. Let us use, for example, shadow plays or photographs.

Our first attempts might focus on observing the human face in its movement from a head-on view to the profile. Observe where 'the nose is looking', not the eyes. Common problem in children's drawing is that they do not realise that

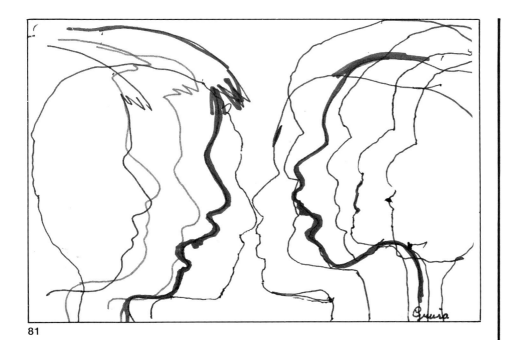

81

81 *Producing two profiles in stages.* One boy placed his head on a sheet of paper, lying on a desk, and another boy traced his profile with a vertically held pencil. In this manner records of conversations in their individual stages were made, such as: 'Look up at that tree', 'How we had an argument, and who won', 'What we were laughing about'.

the nose seems to 'shift away' from the face as the head gradually turns. The axis of the face shifts. We talked about shadow play in the previous chapter where it involved drawing a simple hand-gesture in stages. Now we place 'a model' with a striking profile between a table lamp and a sheet of paper. We can see the first stage in which the shadow of the model appears on the edge of the paper – the profile of the nose appears rather indistinctly and we trace its outline. We repeat the drawing in tiny shifts, stage by stage, until we get a clear profile.

A boy is drawing his friend's shadow in profile. The friend sits in front of a sheet of paper affixed vertically. A lamp situated in the front casts a shadow of the model's head on the paper. It is also possible to place the model behind the paper, and project the light from the rear.

82

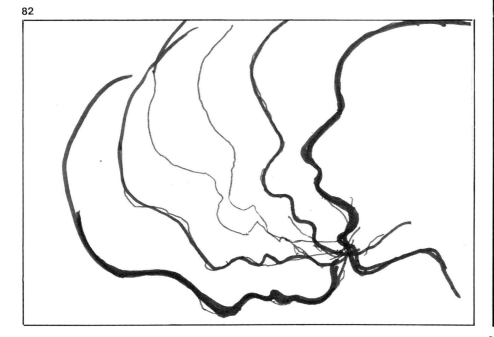

82 *Individual stages of a face pantomime.* There are various types of 'shadow play'. Children try to capture the individual stages of a profile in the process of, e.g., yawning, showing amazement, nodding in agreement, shouting. Each stage of a movement or a grimace should be carefully traced on the paper.

60

83 *Portraits in profile.* Children working in pairs drew each other's portraits. They traced a shadow – the outline of their friend's head in profile, complete with hair. Afterwards, they carefully drew the eyes, ears, and the lines surrounding the nose and the mouth. When drawing the hair they concentrated on its structure. They paid attention to the position and directions of strands and curls. They also attemped to portray the hairstyle, and to observe proportions in relation to the facial area.

Make sure that the children realise that the eyes' position depends on the axis of the face, which may shift.

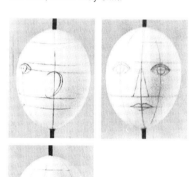

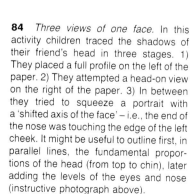

84 *Three views of one face.* In this activity children traced the shadows of their friend's head in three stages. 1) They placed a full profile on the left of the paper. 2) They attempted a head-on view on the right of the paper. 3) In between they tried to squeeze a portrait with a 'shifted axis of the face' – i.e., the end of the nose was touching the edge of the left cheek. It might be useful to outline first, in parallel lines, the fundamental proportions of the head (from top to chin), later adding the levels of the eyes and nose (instructive photograph above).

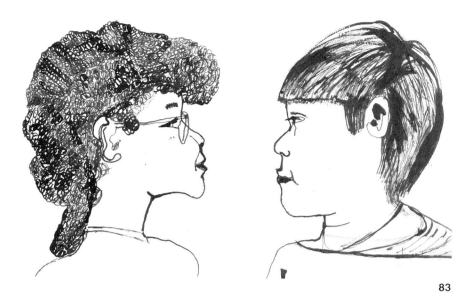

83

Children are likely to enjoy this activity and may be encouraged to 'capture' their whole family in shadow plays and stage by stage drawings. They will then have in their collections not only profiles of their brothers and sisters but also profiles of grandfathers with beards, mothers in Sunday hats, and so on. If children display and arrange these profiles facing one another, they can re-enact conversations, head movements and gestures in different stages (picture 81).

Children might draw the shadow of a whole head in profile and complete the

84

85

85 *The twins.* Two children found an interesting big face in a magazine, and cut it in two parts. Each child glued his part to the middle of his paper. Then each tried to complete the missing part of the face by drawing. The children were able to compare the resulting portraits of the 'twins'. Whether the 'twins' looked like each other or not, the children realised that they could not simplify the nose by drawing only a stick, or the eye by drawing only a circle. Children can also attempt this exercise on their own.

Even though a person's head does not resemble the shape of an egg, it is instructive to note in the accompanying photographs where the nose, the eyes or the chin are situated when we observe the human head from below or from above.

portrait of the model. As they draw the head to scale they can observe the distance from the eye to the base of the nose, and the shape of the upper and lower lips. They can draw the upper edge of the ear in line with the eye and judge its size.

If children make their task of drawing the head simpler by tracing the outline of the shadow they might be willing to tackle the more demanding task of drawing a school friend from three view-points (picture 84).

We recommended children first draw a portrait in profile so as to discover 'how big is the brain area'. If we trace the whole head the cranial area is bigger than the facial area of the head. However, children usually draw the facial area bigger, as they consider it to be 'more important'. They might, now, also notice that adults seem to have their eyes placed slightly higher in the face than children. It is through gradual development and the unequal growth of various areas of the head that the individual achieves 'an adult appearance'.

The Twins is an interesting activity during which children will realise that in a head-on view all noses do not simply look like sticks and all eyes like circles beneath arches. *The Twins* is a collage completed by a drawing. The caption gives full instructions on how to proceed.

A visit to a mirror maze is good fun for children. Mirrors with distorted surfaces reflect a deformed image of the human face. The shiny metal surface of a tea pot may also distort the image of the human face. Children like pulling faces at their 'changed' appearance. Parts of the face stretch unevenly in a distorted mirror as if we were moving our facial muscles in a certain manner. A mime artist in performance can control the facial muscles to an extraordinary extent. Without uttering a word or a sound he is able to elongate his face and his lower lip in an expression of crying. He expresses his happiness by

86 *The distorting mirror*. Children again found an interesting face in a magazine and cut it into narrow vertical or horizontal strips. They glued these strips onto paper in the correct order but slightly shifted. The face appeared to undulate as in a distorting mirror. Thus, the face – by its expression or grimace – reminded the children of a certain mood (a, c). They tried to draw it on another sheet of paper (b), or they emphasised the main features of the face on the distorted picture using Indian ink (d).

a

b

86

opening his eyes wide, raising his mouth. Let some of the children try 'a face pantomime' while others guess what is being mimed – anger, surprise, sadness, disappointment, pride, arrogance, deep thought. Draw children's attention to the facial muscles involved in such grimaces, and the way in which they operate.

The human face is not as symmetrical as it looks at first sight. If we want to see our symmetrical portrait composed from our left cheeks we need two mirrors. We make a little dot on our left cheek. We hold a small rectangular

c

d

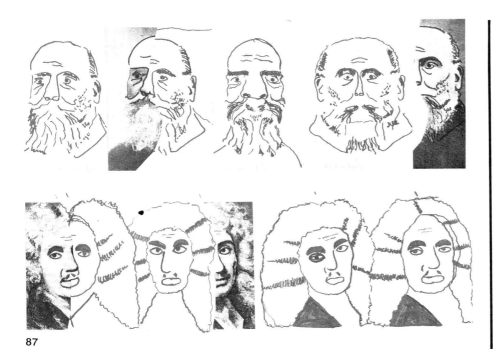

87

87 *A portrait composed from only the right or left cheeks.* In this activity the children cut the photograph of a face out of a magazine, and cut it vertically in half. They put a piece of thin paper over the left cheek and traced its outline against the light of a lamp or a glass pane. They drew the fundamental characteristics of the face in a thicker black felt-tip pen. They then turned the picture of the left cheek upside down, and copied it against the light. They placed it next to their first drawing. Thus, they acquired a symmetrical portrait composed from the left cheeks only. They repeated this creative activity with the picture of the right cheek.

hand-mirror at right angles to the vertical axis of the face and look in the second large mirror. We can see ourselves with two dots on the face if we use our left eye only. You can repeat this experiment with the mirror reflection of your right cheek. If children decide to have more fun in seeing themselves with a beard they can put the hand mirror lengthwise just under the eyes and observe themselves in the large mirror. They can acquire a wrinkle by drawing

88

88 *Light tones, dark tones and semi-tones in the human face* can be observed in the following activity. Children placed a piece of thin paper on a black and white photograph against the light – for example, a window pane – and coloured the lightest spots in yellow felt-tip pen. In the second stage they coloured all the dark surfaces in blue. The remaining surfaces, i.e., semi-tones, were completed in red, as neither dark nor light colours matched their luminosity.

A boy 'changed' his face using a small mirror. He tried to find out if a beard would suit him; he also created his portrait composed from the right cheeks only and observed himself simultaneously in a large mirror.

89 *Human nature reflected in fables.* The children looked at faces in photographs and pointed out which features reminded them of specific animal characteristics. If a broad bearded face topped with plentiful hair reminded them of a lion, the children enriched and emphasised the dishevelled hair and beard. In other pictures they decided to sharpen the nose if it reminded them of a beak; to make the eyes narrower; or to add a bristling moustache. Thus, the person in the photograph acquired the distinctive physiognomy of the proverbial 'cunning fox', 'furious tiger', 'agile cat', 'timid mouse', 'wise owl', 'self-important crow', 'croaking frog', 'majestic lion', or 'cuddly kitten'. The illustrations are not caricatures, but rather examples of typical characteristics found in human faces. Can children recognise which animals these illustrations attempt to depict?

a) Master Lion b) Mr Lion c) Master Cat d) Mr Cat e) Mr Crow f) The Timid Mouse

89   a

b

c

d

e

f

90   In these illustrations the procedure was reversed and a human portrait was obtained from the picture of an owl or a lion by toning down animal features.

a) The Fierce Tiger b) The Old Tiger c) The Cunning Mouse d) Mr Frog e) The Elegant Mr Fox f) Mr Monkey

90   **a**   **b**

Children used in turn a block of wood, a pen and a thin brush.

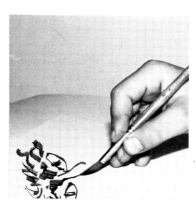

                        c   **d**

                        e   **f**

91 *Exchanging people's hats.* A policeman's helmet, a king's crown, a cook's hat, a bowler hat – hats often tell us what a person's occupation is. The children cut out photographs of various people and interesting 'head-gear' from magazines. They placed unlikely hats on unlikely heads. They observed that this activity often changed expressions on faces!

91

a deep line on their forehead, which in the mirror reflection becomes a mouth. Their hair suddenly becomes a rich beard, which can even be combed. We can play similar magical tricks by combining the mirror with larger photographs. If we turn the mirror slightly the face widens or narrows, the mouth gets bigger or the eyes seem further apart. Children can use photographs of their relatives, famous actors, faces from magazines. Observing and then drawing the changes which occur is a worthy exercise as children will, subconsciously, perceive the structure of the face and its new expression.

As the old saying goes: 'When we are young we have a face given to us by Nature; when we are grown-up our face reflects what we try to look like; and when we are old we get the face we deserve.' This saying is often taken into account by psychologists and used by artists when they draw portraits. They judge a person's character and personality from his face – from his 'fixed

92 *Jules Verne's portrait.* A boy interpreted a photograph of this famous French writer in a strong line, and by contrasting the surfaces of the black coat and the beard. The boy wrote notes to accompany his picture: 'I wish Jules Verne had been my uncle. I'd love to have appeared in his novels. I'd love to have met Captain Nemo and his crew.'

Jules Verne's portrait

92

physiognomic expression'. Our lives, our education, and even frequent repetition of a certain expression (remember the experiment with smiling, anger, surprise, arrogance or deep thought) mark the human face forever. The facial muscles 'become accustomed and fixed' in to a certain expression.

If children select some interesting photographs of human faces they can attempt to draw 'types', somebody as 'cunning as a fox', and somebody as 'timid as a mouse'.

Free drawings based on the photographs of famous personalities may lead to life-size portraits, without intentional copying involved. Children are keen to

93 *Portraits of interesting uncles*. The children's desire to have an adult friend found an expression in the texts and drawings beside 'uncles'' heads, or in hats. They explained how the 'uncle' was interesting; what he was able to do; what he might talk about with them; and also how he could keep them amused and busy. The most sought-after uncles were magicians and inventors; the authors of fairy tales and detective stories; sailors and travellers; and in fact all those who had interesting hobbies (anglers, painters, stamp collectors).

93

create 'a gallery of interesting uncles', whose fantastic hats contain everything that they wish adults would give them. Our illustrations and captions explain which 'uncles' were the most desirable. Their jobs and occupations very often revealed the children's own secret wishes.

A

B

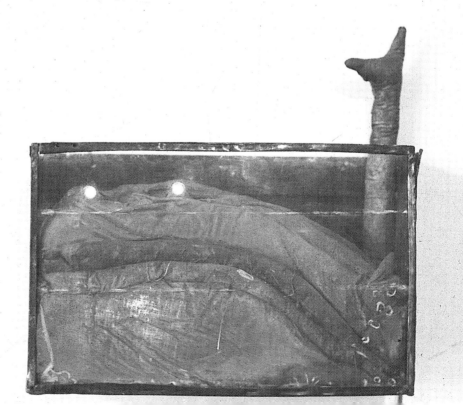

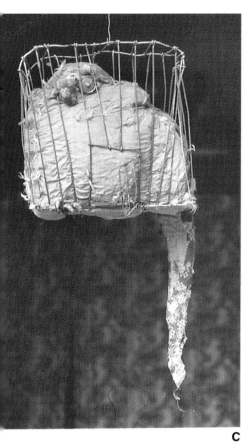

C

A *A Rock Reflection in Water*
Josef Čapek, the Czech painter, once said:
'You can see an old man in all elderly men, but
also in younger men and children, in a flying
bird, in the autumn wind . . . Everything in the
world contains elements of man.' Thus, it is also
possible to envisage a human face in the rock's
surface glittering in water.

B Kurt Gebauer (b. 1941)
'A Well-Fed Fish', canvas, 1974, plexi-glass,
40 × 40 cm

C Kurt Gebauer (b. 1941)
'Hypertrophied Parrot', 1973, canvas, metal,
feathers, 70 × 30 cm
These 'poor little things' might have disinte-
grated had it not been for their cages into which
they 'spread', thanks to our misplaced care.
They exchanged their free movement through
the air or water for this enforced 'well-being'.
Now, they are neither fish nor fowl. They might
even be portraits of people. But what sort of
people do they portray?

D Václav Stratil (b. 1950)
'Black Head', 1987, drawing in Indian ink on
paper, 270 × 150 cm
It seems that tiny, carefully arranged lines on
paper approximately three metres in length,
express the artist's desire not to 'hurry'. It looks
as if he were proving himself and demonstrating
his ability to concentrate – his physical strength.

D

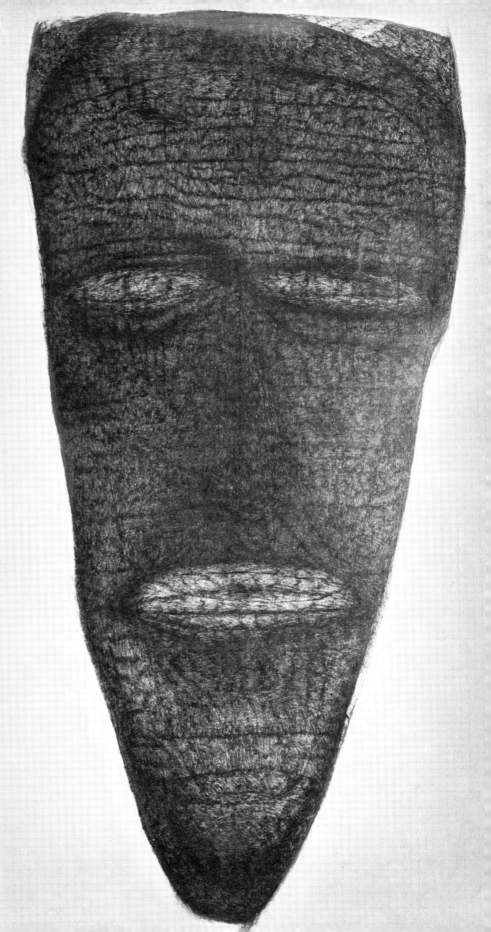

6

95

The Natural World

In the beginning there was a stone. Water as the source of life. The mysteries of plant structure. Creating a beetle. A shell's hidden secret. Cats and rabbits. Fantastic animals.

---

94 *The portrayal of Mother Nature.* Before drawing a colour portrait the children made a model – a puppet on which they put many natural objects, e.g., sea shells, egg shells, feathers, dried flowers, necklaces made from berries or rose hips. The children then created their drawing of Mother Nature, and completed it with cutouts of a landscape from a magazine or calendar.

95 *How a butterfly's wings are formed within the pupa.* The children first imagined that Indian ink soaked into a wet sheet of paper represented an enlarged, mysterious place where a butterfly lived. As the ink and paper gradually dried, the children created beautiful butterfly wings by spreading coloured paints on the randomly appearing grey surfaces. They finished the details of the wings with coloured felt-tip pens when the paper was dry. You can ask the children if they have ever seen a pupa. They could observe it through a magnifying glass. Is it not, indeed, one of the wonders of Nature that such delicate butterfly wings can be concealed within such a tiny space?

Children are lucky. They see everything that surrounds them in the natural world in a fresh light. Their ecological habits, whether good or bad, are ingrained when they are very small. If children are guided in their discoveries by a sensitive adult they gradually formulate the equation: Observe – discover – draw – make friends = No destruction of Nature. Let us attempt to observe Nature through children's eyes, as if for the first time, and attempt to contribute to their understanding of the links between animate and inanimate Nature.

The biological evolution of life on Earth has taken approximately 3500 billion years. Countless animal and plant species are endowed with ingenious bodily structures and methods of sustaining life. We should discourage children from drawing only the surfaces of natural objects. We should satisfy children's curiosity using nature books, photographs, a magnifying glass or a microscope. Let us answer the children's questions, such as: 'Why is a pebble round?'; 'How does a butterfly emerge from a pupa?'; 'Why has a butterfly got coloured wings?'; 'How does a butterfly see?'; 'Why does a rabbit

73

96

96 *A limestone with quartz veins* is freely 'transcribed' in an interesting line, using Indian ink and a block of wood. Before children started to draw, they spread colour chalk with their fingers in order to achieve the colour tone of the stone's surface. If the stone has an interesting uneven surface children might like to use the technique of rubbing as well. Thus, the quartz veins come to the surface as secret writing, recounting what the stone has 'witnessed'.

change the colour of its fur?'; 'Why can an ant not live on its own?'. Our explanations might be given in the form of a legend, a fable or a fairy tale.

Let us start with an ordinary pebble. In fact, we hold in our hand primaeval matter out of which Earth itself was formed. What did this little stone witness before it separated from its parent rock? How did it find its way to a sand-pit or a path? Children become enthusiastic collectors when we take them to the heaps of assorted gravel in a disused quarry or to the banks of a shallow stream. Let us help them with their collecting. Stones can be collected according to shape, colour or surface markings. Back home these can be kept in jars filled with water and placed against the light. Such an arrangement enhances their beauty. Another time we might announce a 'treasure hunt' for a stone statue, or a stone with magical marks, or a stone striped like a tiger. Interesting shapes somehow 'beg' to be drawn. We can also find inspiration in

Snowflakes have beautiful regular six-sided shapes. The six-sided 'bricks' appear to have an extremely solid structure. We come across them in honeycombs, too. ▶

97

97 *A landscape built from a small stone.* By drawing only one stone with an uneven surface the children reminded themselves that their small model was originally part of a massive parent mountain. By turning the stone and drawing it from several angles, and connecting the individual drawings, it was possible to create an entire mountain ridge. The children completed this stony landscape through collage.

74

98 *What happens in a drop of water?* Before starting their work the children reminded themselves of the Slavonic fairy tale motif of 'The Water of Life and Death'. First, the children drew the Water of Life in Indian ink on a sheet of paper. In the middle of the drawing a spring bubbles, and it spreads round in 'jolly' ripples. The children added tone to the drawing with colour, and created the simple shapes of micro-organisms which live in water, even in the tiniest drop.

98

a geological atlas filled with brightly coloured illustrations of minerals, semi-precious and precious stones.

Water – whether in the form of an ocean, a flowing river, a spring, a humble puddle, a rain drop or a snowflake – protects all living organisms on our planet. Water formed the primaeval soup in which living organisms first appeared and ever since it has nourished them. Observing the shapes formed by water is fascinating. Water can be perceived by all our five senses. We can make discoveries everywhere – standing on the bank of a pond; observing a puddle

99

99 *How Nature invented the water spider.* This work was made as a drawing on a differently coloured wet surface. In the dark depths of the ocean, Nature had enough time to invent fantastical shapes of eyes, mouths, and tentacles, and to decide through biological evolution which would be the most appropriate. Children can attempt a drawing which uses a real spider's web as its model. It is also possible to make a huge spider's web in Nature, using strings tied among trees.

100

100 *Looking into a bunch of flowers.*
A bunch of flowers in a vase seems to be merely one plant composed of many blossoms. It is possible to draw small details in a fine line, while a stronger line can be used to depict the construction of the stems, leaves and blossoms. The children observed a bunch of flowers from above. Their drawings gradually widened, and could be halted whenever they wished.

In the chart you can see the characteristics of various trees. Could you express verbally how these trees differ – e.g., in their height, the shape of their tops, the length of their trunks, the arrangement of their branches. Could you identify these trees?

formed by the rain; or even observing a puddle depicted on a sheet of paper. How can we reproduce the waves whipped up by the wind or rapids cascading down a river bed? How can we include imaginary creatures and plants on the surface of 'moving water' drawn on paper? Our illustrations may help to answer these questions.

What do we know of the first plants on Earth's surface? They appeared over 400 million years ago. If we want to see what the first miniature forest might have looked like let us examine a patch of moss through a magnifying glass.

We can observe one plant – for example, a dandelion – and draw it complete with roots. However, we discover more by comparing several plants. Let us compare drawings of a stick of celery, a horse radish, a carrot and a turnip as one group; potatoes and chrysanthemums' bulbs might belong to a second group; a third group might consist of onion, garlic and tulip bulbs. We can learn more by comparing the shapes and structures of root systems. Similarly, we can compare the structural differences of these plants above ground level. We might observe the shapes and arrangement of leaves and types of floral patterns – symmetrical or rounded (dandelion, poppy, sweet pea, iris). It is also interesting to compare the shapes of soft fruits and dry seeds. Children might dry plants for a collection. For creative activities it is useful if plants are placed between two panes of glass. By putting their drawings against the glass, children can make alterations. We should encourage children to have a plant atlas on their book shelves at home. Their initial interest in drawing plants may eventually lead to a serious interest in biology. If children decide to draw a fantastic giant plant on the pavement in chalk, then let them do it. It is the privilege of both an artist and a child to invent new plant shapes, as Nature has done over the ages.

101 *Trees resemble human beings* in the shape of their tops, or through the breadth or narrowness of their trunks. Their branches, like human hands, can convey agitated or calm gestures. We might suggest to children the image of a bride while standing in front of an apple tree covered with white blossoms; the image of a veiled weeping lady while standing in front of a weeping willow tree; or the image of a heavy-weight champion while standing in front of an oak tree. Our illustrations are intended as puzzles. What did the children want to say about the characteristics or moods of a particular tree in their drawings? They used finer or thicker lines in order to emphasise certain features of a tree. They also used creative means to underline characteristic features.

a) The Bride b) Two Fighters c) Mothers d) The Witch

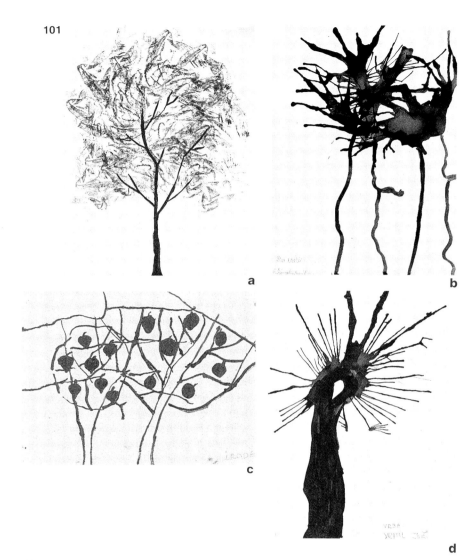

101

a

b

c

d

Trees have been on Earth since time immemorial and the relationship between trees and people is of long standing. Trees provided the first shelter and protection for mankind. Timber was used as fuel and as a building material. As we know from myths, legends and fairy tales, trees were venerated as sacred objects. How amazing it is that a graft or a tiny seed has the potential to grow into, for example, an apple tree. However, if trees were able to run, nowadays they would probably run a mile from us! But is there anywhere for them to hide from our newly found 'relationship' with herbicides? There is nothing more disheartening than watching trees die. Let us draw trees without foliage. Let us have a look under their bark. In our illustrations we attempt to consider the nature of a tree and its resemblance to a human being. Would it not be marvellous if every father took his son up to a tree and told him: 'Look, this tree is the same age as you are. I planted it when you were born. Remember that, and become good friends, you two!'

Plants and insects have a close relationship, too. They need one another. Plants vie with one another in attracting insects, using the shape and colour of

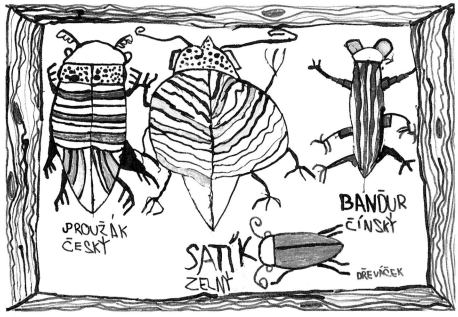

102

102 *A collection of fantastic beetles.* The children drew several large beetles simultaneously. They drew their axis of symmetry, and thus determined their fundamental measurements and position on the paper. They then gradually invented the three fundamental sections of the beetles' bodies, in scales of both size and shape. Firstly, they drew the head with its sense organs (i.e., the compound eyes), and the fantastic shape of its jaws and antennae. Secondly, they attempted the thorax with its organs of movement, i.e., the three pairs of articulated legs and one or two pairs of wings or hard sheaths. Finally, they drew the abdomen, which contains the internal organs, and which is partially enclosed by the wings or sheaths. The children gained inspiration for their 'fantastic beetles' from an atlas of beetles and from sketches made during a field trip. The work was completed by adding a two-name classification based on the characteristic shape, food, habitat, and behaviour – for example, 'antroach', 'ladywig', 'earbird'.

their flowers and their scent. After all, a butterfly can see the world in colour, and a bee has a well-developed olfactory sense. The structure of insect bodies and their senses are ingenious and complex. Nature has 'created' over 700,000 million types of known insects, and there may very well be many more waiting to be discovered. Children would undoubtedly be terrified by a dragonfly with a half-metre wing span! However, such dragonflies did exist over 300 million years ago. Children may need a magnifying glass and a small transparent plastic box for their discoveries. They can carefully 'hunt' for tiny specimens in the grass and in bushes, and having drawn them, they can return them to Nature. If children are drawing a beetle, we suggest that it be magnified several times. They can start by drawing only the symmetrical half of the beetle's body along its perpendicular axis; from the top, bottom and in its three fundamental sections, including all anatomical details. Let us remember that all types of insects display a three-part basic anatomical structure – head, thorax and abdomen. If children succeed in observing insects correctly, they can 'invent' other beetles based on this structure (picture 102).

People have always envied the insects and birds their ability to fly. Bird feathers – one of Nature's most ingenious designs – are able to provide warmth and camouflage; they identify individual species by colour and shape; and, finally, they enable birds to fly. A fossilised feather over five centimetres long was discovered in limestone in Bavaria. It belonged to a primaeval bird which had some reptilian features and lived approximately 140 million years ago. When children draw and later construct a bird using egg shells and feathers, they might mount the shells on a piece of wood and glue the feathers onto them. Thus, they can create a memorial to all birds, from a tiny wren to a three metre extinct moa.

A city child is not likely to be afraid of a cat, a dog or even a tiger. However, a close encounter with a cow might scare the city child, despite our

Let children try to create the simplified shape of a beetle or a butterfly using the familiar folding technique. We know that the beetle and the butterfly are symmetrical along their axis. It is sufficient to paint one half of the body and – while still wet – print this on the paper folded along the axis. We use a paint squeezed directly out of a tube. The image will be more striking if we also employ a clean roller.

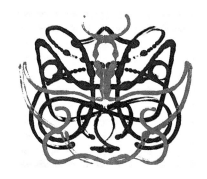

103

103 *A bird's feather*. Impressions of a feather were made by dipping it in colour, and by rubbing it, before drawing it in pencil (and later in Indian ink). As the feather is asymmetrical along its shaft it is necessary to judge accurately the fundamental shape and directions of the feather's filaments.

104 *What hatched from the shell* is not a particularly impressive bird, not exactly a majestic monarch of the air! This is a nestling with a few feathers, which can do very little. The children tore the basic shape of the featherless body from coloured paper, and attempted to draw several feathers from memory.

104

105

106

105 *The design of a coloured tiger* is, in fact, a photograph from a magazine which the children completed with coloured felt-tip pens. This is based on the time-honoured custom of adorning pictures to pass the time when reading. This activity is, perhaps, a subconscious effort to view the familiar in a new light; in colour; in a new context; and in a humorous manner. This is not very surprising if we recall that people also adorn their bodies. This can be witnessed in ritualistic face painting by primitive tribes, and in advertising by chemists' shops of chic and fashionable cosmetics.

assurances that this animal provides milk for breakfast. Let us, therefore, remain with beasts of prey – affectionate domesticated cats! Cats are accessible for children's observation and study. A cat does not usually mind if it is the object of children's attention, even for a long time. We can record the cat's soft purring and draw its shape on a sheet of paper. If we stroke the cat it will remain spread-eagled on the floor. We can even ask the cat 'to do us a favour' and walk on paper with its paws coloured with chalk. This will allow children to study the cat's paw-prints. Finally, we can comb the cat's fur – we draw the comb through the fur, not the wrong way as the cat would not like it. Later, children can start drawing the cat (illustrations on page 80).

Rabbits and hares do not enjoy an easy life in Nature. They are not spoiled

107

106, 107 *Drawings of cats.* The children portrayed a cat in a certain mood or action. They combed a purring and happy cat. They also bristled the fur on the back of an angry cat, using several brush strokes.

108 *A rabbit.* This drawing is based on a photograph of a real rabbit. It did not involve a simple tracing. Children were asked to transcribe the delicate rabbit fur creatively. They could not possibly depict every single hair. They had to decide on their own approach. Nevertheless, they did observe the delicacy and direction of the fur.

108

109

like cats. In order to ensure their survival, Nature has endowed them, firstly, with long ears which give them excellent hearing; secondly, with long hind legs which allow them to run fast and in a zig-zag fashion; and thirdly, with very good camouflage. (Incidentally, have you read Richard Adams' animal tale *Watership Down?* – If you have, you must have made friends with its rabbit heroes.) We can express our sympathies towards these species which are, in

110

109, 110 *Photomontage,* i.e., what was designed in order that a rabbit might fly. The children added to the original photograph those features which might enable the rabbit to escape. They used collage. The rabbit could become a butterfly with the long legs of a deer, or it could become a grouse or even an eagle. The children did not add drawings to these photomontages.

81

111

A fantastic zoo (or pages from a fantastic bestiary) also provides various technical methods of approach. Depending on their choice, the children can create fantastic animals by drawing in black and white with a block of wood, or by shading in colour. In order to express the animal fur, children can employ a brush, or the techniques of collage and photomontage based on cut-outs from magazines or calendars.

111 *The Butterfly Squirrel,* drawing with a block of wood and a brush

fact, being persecuted by 'civilised man'. We might 'invent' something, something which would make them less vulnerable. Using the technique of collage children might endow them with wings, longer hind legs or even antlers (illustrations on page 81).

We have no time to mention every creature here, but we should encourage children to create a bestiary of fantastic animals, possessing feathers, furs, scales, different beaks, crests, antlers, trunks, spines, hoofs, claws, fins or

112

112 *The Horsey Lamb,* drawing with a block of wood and a sharp-tipped brush

113 *The Long-eared Fish,*
drawing with a block of wood and a fine-
tipped brush

113

tails. We could hold a competition for drawing or making collages of an animal which has as many parts from different species as possible. Children can find inspiration in a nature book or recall their last visit to the zoo. The children's 'fantastic bestiary' might contain a two-name classification of individual animals, a description of the bodily structure and habitat. Children should also indicate whether a particular 'new' animal could survive for any length of time in Nature.

114

114 *The Camel with a Trunk,*
drawing with a block of wood completed in
coloured inks and felt-tip pens

A

D

A *Hoar frost* and its fragile beauty on the tufts of grass or branches attracts a passer-by's attention and makes him walk on tip-toes.

B *A pupa,* one of the butterfly's metamorphoses, is an excellent shape – full of purpose; a structure which is modelled from the inside by the ingenious spatial accommodation of the butterfly's folded wings and body. Children mentioned that inside the pupa a bird, a frog, even a dragon could be hidden. Could the children design a comfortable 'pupa' for themselves?

C *Egg shells* are rather interesting when light and shade fall on them. They are well worth drawing; modelling with a flexible wire or a skewer; gluing together; or even inserting inside one another to form an endless cylinder.

D *Zebras* can also be viewed differently; e.g., as large striped beans before sprouting; huge snakes' heads;

E

fantastic amphibious fish; or even 'cunning' conches.

E Ivan Kafka (b. 1952)
'Seven Stone Piles for the Town of Stein', medium: marble – Carrara, Giallo mori, Rosso Verona, Marone, Verde alpi, Schremser; hard coal; height 160 cm, width 400 cm, length 2900 cm, weight 56 tonnes
We pass piles of stone, gravel, or sand without noticing them. However, here we suddenly appreciate their beauty and wider implications. The piles attract us by the unity of their conic shapes; even a single stone in each pile has its indispensable place, as if it were part of a larger organism.

F Jaromír Rybák (b. 1952)
'Barrier' ('Dragon's teeth'), glued-glass sculpture, 175 × 60 cm
Glass black thorns grow from the earth, where they seem to derive their secret, dangerous germinal shape.

F

7

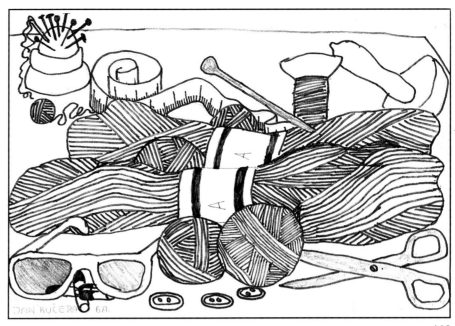

116

The World of Objects

Cotton reels, wool yarn, textiles and knots. Keys and workshop tools. Paper toys. How we look at building blocks. How we draw a cylinder.

Let us ask the children to imagine that, suddenly, overnight, all ordinary objects like buttons, threads, keys, hammers, scissors, handbags, mugs and chairs have disappeared. We would soon discover that without these seemingly humble objects we could not visualise our world. These objects 'co-exist' with us. Years ago someone must have invented them for us; since then they have been gradually improved and now they seem permanent. Even if we attempt to improve handles in order to make them more sophisticated; or to manufacture thinner thread; or to update handbag designs, the fundamental functions of these objects do not change. If these objects meet our needs, or their shapes are convenient and their colours are pleasing to our eye, then they are acceptable. We could hardly drive in a nail with anything more ingenious than a hammer. We could not knit a jersey or a pair of gloves with anything more perfect than woollen yarn. Would it be more satisfying to drink coffee out of anything other than a mug? It is obvious that these humble objects do deserve to be drawn. Children should try to draw

115 *Objects from Mother's sewing box.* The children had in front of them ribbons of various colours and widths, buckles, safety pins and so on. The ribbons were important for practising drawing objects in space. The children started to draw the first ribbon in pencil. It was limited by two lines at its edges. The children carefully observed the same width of the ribbon but they soon discovered that when turned the ribbon became narrower; its bottom edge disappeared and then appeared again. Therefore, the children had to draw in fine lines the part that was invisible as well. They then traced everything that was visible with a coloured felt-tip pen. They were able to imagine what was above and what was below. Finally, they tied all the ribbons onto a seamstress's portrait.

116 *Cotton balls and wool yarn.* The children first outlined in pencil the cotton balls which were the nearest, starting from the bottom of the paper, and then those balls behind them. They then drew with a block of wood dipped in Indian ink; some children used felt-tip pens. It was rather difficult not to 'tear wool' – i.e., the lines – and to express the difference between the tightly reeled cotton and the loosely arranged wool fibres.

87

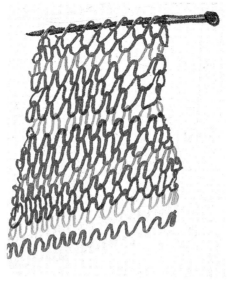

117

118

them as they stand – a cotton reel merits a dignified uninterrupted line. Our drawings should show that a hammer exists to be worked with; that a chair is to be sat in; that a mug is for drinking out of. How do we, in fact, view these objects?

Before children start to make more complex drawings of objects in space, they have to start thinking logically and exercise their eyes and their hand while drawing simple objects observed from above (basket cane, a bunch of keys) or objects whose parts are juxtaposed (cotton reels, ribbons, knots).

119

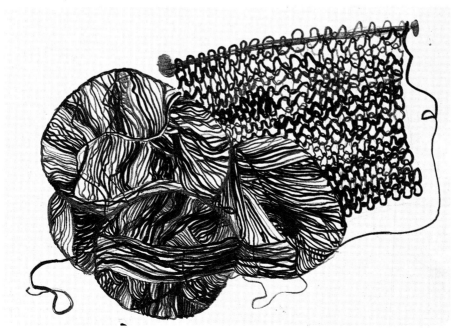

We should check regularly that the children are holding the instruments correctly (not clamped in an inflexible wrist); that they do not peer too closely at their drawings, and that they sit with straight backs. We should also consider whether the light is suitable.

118, 119 *Grandmother's knitting.* Here the technique adopted was the same as in the introductory illustration. Knitting is another means of observing the structure of wool. The individual rows interloop, and the wool forms a continuous line. If we want to trace a long and steady line, it is necessary to be skilful and patient when dipping a block of wood in Indian ink.

120, 121 *American Indians' system of string writing.* Here the technique adopted when making the drawing was similar to the individual stages of making a model. The children first pencilled the basic loop, onto which they tied additional strings. The strings can interconnect with or without knots. By shifting three to four model knots we get other variants. At first the children can draw what is invisible in pencil. They can then draw the entire tangle as it is observed in space, using a thicker line in felt-tip pen. The children might enlarge some knots at the edge of the paper, making them as big as a sailor's bowline. You can notice that by such enlargement it is also possible to portray those threads which make up the rope, and by shadowing to express its special surfaces.

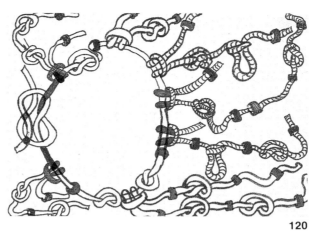

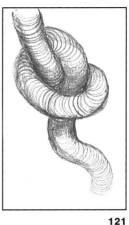

120

121

Thus, children soon realise that to observe and to draw an object is a matter of routine. They discover that visual drawing has its definite stages: estimating the proportions of the whole object; estimating the scale of individual objects; the axis of symmetry; the foreshortening in space – i. e., the distorting effects. We will discuss these effects later.

Let us now imagine what cotton reels or waving ribbons look like in space, including the concealed parts. The children might like to draw in pencil that which is 'invisible'. (The children should ensure that one cotton reel is not taking up another's space; that individual reels are placed next to each other; that they do not float in the air.) We try to approach drawing as fun. If the children felt bored or complained that 'drawing was too difficult for them', then

122 *Happy hoses.* The children soon realised what the space was in this drawing of a tangle of 'corridors and tunnels'. This is a drawing puzzle for which the children used a small template – i.e., either a triangle or a circle (coins or buttons). They moved the template on the paper and partially traced it with a felt-tip pen. Some children decided to outline the directions of the curves in pencil, and then moved the template according to these pencil directions.

122

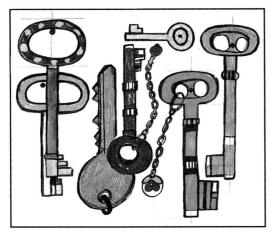

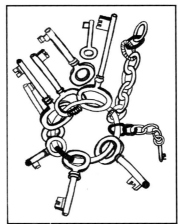

123   **124**

123 *Keys which might unlock secrets* were drawn by younger children. These are fantastic images of keys as far as colour and partial shapes are concerned. Nevertheless, it would be possible to unlock a door using such keys because they have a suitable length, a functional point and indentations.

124 *A key ring.* The children drew keys in pencil from a model, like the knots. They started with fine lines. Then, relying on their knowledge of what is visible and what is invisible, they drew imagined keys onto the key-ring. In order to assist their memory they enlarged some details of the keys at the edge of the paper.

A boy judges particular proportions. He holds a piece of wood vertically, with his arm stretched out. He marks one section with his thumb, and then judges the size of individual parts of the depicted object (e.g., a grinder). He would use a similar procedure when judging the size and proportions of the school bag in picture 126.

all these creative activities would become useless exercises. After all, we are not interested in imitating reality perfectly. We are interested in discovering the secrets of human perspective and unveiling the intrinsic beauty of ordinary objects. Drawing from a model is only one of numerous artistic activities.

Drawing knotted strings is an enjoyable and seemingly simple puzzle. Children might be keen to play with a tangle of knotted strings if we tell them that it is, in fact, an ancient writing system used by American Indians. We can remind children when they start drawing that the thread in a knot is not 'transparent'. It is limited by two lines. We have to rely on our sense of perspective in order that the thread concealed in a knot appears in the correct position (picture 121). The next illustration depicts a similar 'maze' modelled on articulated hoses. Smaller children will manage this activity, too.

A bunch of keys admits us into our home every day. When children realise that they have lost their keys they might feel that just behind their front door is the most perfect and secure spot in the world. It might be quite an interesting

125

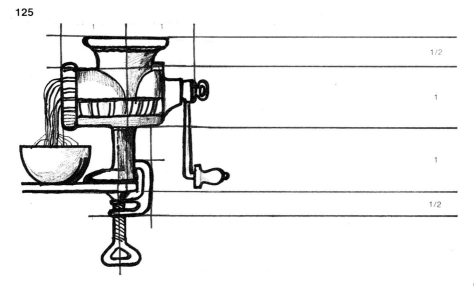

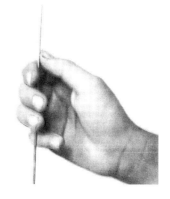

125 *A grinder.* When drawing a grinder it should be imagined as a whole. It is composed of bigger and smaller parts whose sizes are in proportion. However, could the grinder in the drawing function in real life? You can observe its proportions and divisions in the instructive drawing.

126 *The drawing of a school bag* might be easier than the drawing of a grinder. When drawing a school bag, children should keep a distance from it in order to view it as a whole. Firstly, the children judge the bag's proportions (how many times can the height, which is smaller, fit into the width? This proportion can be roughly established through 'visualisation'. The children can be asked to hold a pencil vertically so that they can move their thumb up and down it. They close one eye and 'mark' the height of the school bag on the pencil by the thumb. They then hold the pencil with the 'marked' height parallel to the width of the bag, estimating how many times the height could fit into the width). They can also draw the school bag's pockets, using the vertical axis of symmetry. Later, the children can draw the details in fine line.

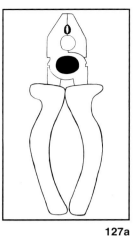

126   127a

experience for children to lose and then find their keys again. They might then realise the value of what is locked away from them. Perhaps, too, they might appreciate the value of their humble keys! The drawing of a bunch of keys heaped on top of each other might remind us of the similar puzzle we experienced when drawing a piece of knotted string. That drawing involved a crooked wavy line. Drawing keys or tools calls for a steady continuous line. All illustrated objects have an axis of symmetry. The children measure the individual components of the objects and try to draw them true to size and scale. They are, however, most interested in drawing objects which would perform a function. Would the key in the drawing unlock the door?

127, 128 *Simple workshop tools*, which mostly have an axis of symmetry, were drawn from above, true to size. Children checked the proportions by placing an object directly onto their drawing. They were most interested in drawing objects which were functional. Is the pair of pliers in the drawing functional? In the next drawing the children tried to show a tool which did not want to be held (127 b). The boys suggested a further activity. They drew their idea of a *universal* tool, similar in design to a multi-purpose can-opener, or a Swiss army knife. The boys joined several tools together, revealing a great deal of constructive imagination.

128   127 **b**

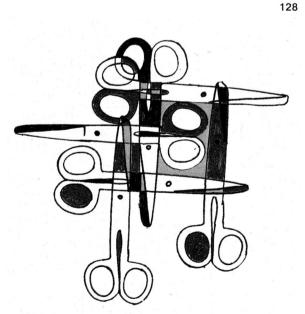

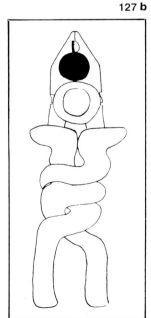

129

130

129 *A maze of paper strips* is a more complex variant of the drawing of ribbons. Children can successfully draw such folded strips, which stand on one edge, if they start from the upper edge. They then draw vertical lines from the folds, and complete the lower edge of the folded paper in the same wide strip. In the beginning, it might even be useful to outline in fine lines what is invisible in the folds. Some children made drawing easier by holding two differently coloured crayons in one hand, keeping them the same distance from one another. By this trick they were able to draw both edges of the paper strip simultaneously. Other children, who were worried that they might lose their way in the maze, prepared two-colour strips (for example, red on the upper side and blue on the reverse side) as models. They observed which walls of the paper strip could be shaded.

130 In the chart you can also see the illustrations of strips which were lying on the surface, or strips which were turned. Children should observe the strips from one point only!

'For fun', children might attempt to draw a key, a hammer or a screwdriver in such a manner that these objects could not function in real life.

Paper toys, which are basically just simple folded and rolled up strips of paper, improve children's imaginative grasp of space. This effect is even more profound if children also attempt to draw these toys. Children realise that a sheet of paper suddenly gives rise to a shape, i.e., a space limited by interesting walls. Using paper strips it is possible to make furniture (a table with chairs, shelves or a bed); the area of a town square; street lay-outs; climbing frames and slides in a playground; or even a maze. It is necessary to develop an imaginative grasp of space even for making the surface drawing of an object. Therefore, children should have enough time for folding up strips of paper and for spatial designs. Anyone who has experienced the magic of origami – the Japanese art of folding up paper into decorative forms and toys – is aware of the constructive imagination and the numerous variations involved.

These decorative forms and toys seem to link logic in their construction and emotion in their design. They make an adult playing with children at one with

131, 132 *Ships and boats.* The children first put these paper toys on a sheet of paper and traced their outlines. They discovered that the side of a boat was formed by three similar triangles, and the side of a ship consisted of two incomplete squares. When drawing these objects in space the children observed how these basic geometrical shapes changed when they shifted the toys.

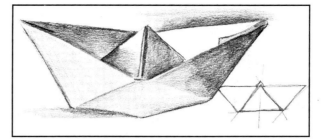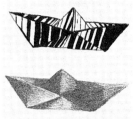

131

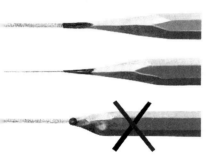

We prefer a soft-leaded pencil when attempting a finely shaded drawing of a smaller object. The pencil may have to be sharpened several times for younger children.

them, and vice versa. It is not only the process of folding paper but the consequent activities which raise the resultant toy into the creative sphere – we can draw folded-up objects and glue them onto a sheet of paper, completing the effect by drawing. These objects can also become more complex models for free but detailed drawing which advances children's ability to observe and draw shapes.

A 'still' or movie camera can magically reproduce on a print or a screen the three-dimensional world of objects in the same manner as our eyes view them. We accept these reproductions happily. A friend walking away appears so small that we can even blot him out with our thumb. A round lid seen sideways appears to be oval. A square table top seems to lose its right angles. However, is human vision the only 'correct' vision? Photographers and cameramen employ optical illusions to let us see objects differently: they produce multi-images of a person similar to those seen by the composite eye of a fly; or a person might be presented in a 'concaved' fashion as if seen

132

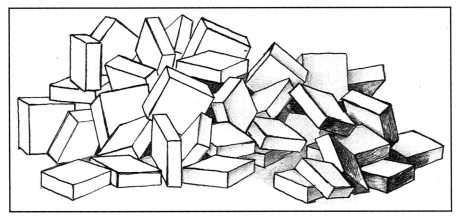

133

The principles of perspective. Imagine viewing toy building blocks through a vertical sheet of glass whose upper end is parallel with the forehead. The level of the eyes is the horizontal line (H). We view from above everything that is below the horizontal line. We view from below everything that is above the horizontal line.

a) All lines and surfaces that are parallel to the sheet of glass are not distorted – a square remains a square, it is a frontal view.

b) All lines and surfaces that are not parallel to the glass are foreshortened.

c) All lines and surfaces that are at right angles to the glass converge into a quadrilateral (in the illustration the centre of a cross – between the eyes).

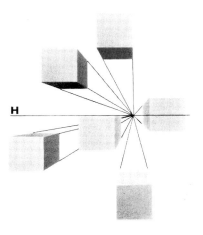

through a fish's eye. Children can also be reminded that doctors make the human body 'transparent' by using X-rays.

Creative artists, and children too, often portray the world independently of customary human vision. In Egyptian paintings events were usually recorded in strips placed one above the other. In early medieval paintings the most important figures were the largest; individual objects simply overlapped one with another while more distant objects were not drawn smaller. In Cubist paintings one artist composed or divided objects on a surface as if he were able to view them from above and from varying angles. Another painter let his figures and objects float freely in space as in a dream. It is, thus, important not to view a painting as if merely through binoculars.

The creative artist depicts the world through his images as freely as he senses and experiences it. However, Renaissance architects, sculptors and painters were the first to become interested in how objects and spaces could be placed in order to convey perspective. Masaccio, the Italian painter of the Early Renaissance, drew his paintings in such a manner that they seem quite natural to us. They portray the world as seen by the human eye. Later, Leonardo da Vinci and Michelangelo wrote theses on the rules of 'perspective vision'. **Perspective** is the technique of drawing – for example wooden bricks, cylinders, mugs and houses – on a plane surface so as to give the same impressions of relative position and magnitude as the actual objects do when viewed from a particular point. Even though we get acquainted with the simple principles of perspective in illustrations we should rely primarily on our own eyes.

134 *Observing a pile of toy bricks.* Children cut out several basic shapes (squares or rectangles) from a thicker sheet of paper before they started to draw a pile of bricks. If they traced the outline of a square, then the square remained undistorted, i.e., it was a frontal view. The two visible side walls of a brick were foreshortened, their lines converging. The children gradually drew other bricks. They drew their positions in an imaginary pile.

134

135

135 The previous drawing depicted the frontal view of the brick sides. In this drawing only the vertical edges of the brick are parallel to the level of the glass. It can be seen from the angle of the deflected brick sides that the lines of the brick edges converge into the left and right quadrilaterals.

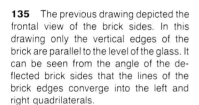

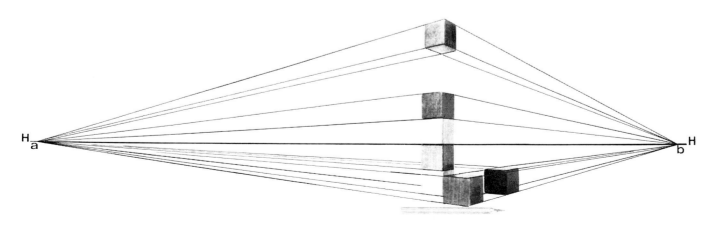

136

136 *A still-life with cylinders and spheres* is shaded, and thus a stronger impression of space is given. The light comes from the left, and changes into semi-shade and shade. The line which originally outlined the shapes should, in fact, disappear. The light, semi-shade and shade now outline the shapes. They should not meet at the interfaces of the shapes.

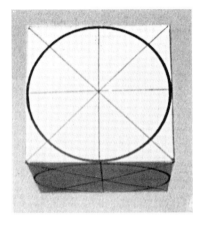

In our illustrations we reduce the world of solid objects to simple prisms and cylinders as found in children's building blocks. If we look carefully we can see that objects can indeed be reduced to these geometrical shapes. Children might find it helpful to use these fundamental shapes in the introductory stages of drawing. We can find boxes, jars or detergent containers at home. We might arrange a still-life using three or four of these objects of different

137

137 *Wooden reels.* The illustration shows that the children were trying to draw a more complex object using the principles of perspective. They also drew defective cylinders on one part of the paper. They understood very well that the eye could not see the objects distorted in this manner. Can you discover those distortions for yourselves?

138 *Good luck buttons* were drawn by small children who observed them from above.

139, 140 *A still-life with fruit jars, or dishes.* The children first discovered where the horizontal plane of the eyes was. There they could see objects from slightly above – i.e., under the horizontal plane. Only skilled artists and those who draw routinely can observe things properly. Nevertheless, we suggest that children observe a still-life as a whole, in which individual objects are in proportion to each other. It might also be helpful to simplify objects into the basic shapes of squares and rectangles, which also helps to differentiate between those objects which are positioned in front, and those which are positioned behind.

138

139

Children can have some fun with the distortion of a circle. We make a large cube and draw or glue circles to its sides. The circles change if we turn the cube in different directions, i.e., if we change the visual angle. Keen observers will notice that the circle on the front is not distorted, whereas on the opposite side the circle is distorted. However, it is neither an oval nor an ellipse, as its closest part is always slightly bigger.

sizes, which children draw from one angle. (We might suggest drawing them from above.) Children draw the details, such as labels or contents of the jars, at the very end. They can draw in soft pencil, charcoal, chalk, Indian ink or using a block of wood.

140

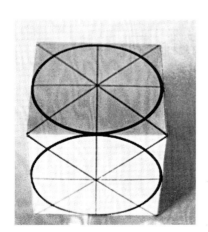

A

B

C

D

A *A pile of regular paving stones.* Let us remind ourselves of the creative activities discussed in this chapter. Paving stones are not arranged symmetrically but heaped randomly. However, none of them float in the air! They are piled one against the other; one stone's position determines that of each adjoining stone. If children want to draw them they will have to be aware of spatial considerations.

B *Pipes.* An infinite maze of cylinders creates an interesting linear rhythm. Would children be able to draw this 'composite scheme'? It is also possible to judge the whole structure's spatial arrangement from linear concentration or separation.

C *A pyrite crystal* is an ingenious spatial structure. Geometric shapes are modelled by light and shade. Differently sized cubic shapes evoke the feeling of tension – a rhythm of mutually balancing shapes, which we can observe in town architecture.

D *Little roots* remind us of the pipes' structure. They might evoke a consideration of spatial interfaces. Could the children try to explain how and in what way the roots differ from the pipes?

E Ivan Kafka (b. 1952)
'Wiring', 1983, hops, wire, 700 × 700 × 900 cm

F Ivan Kafka (b. 1952)
'Common Land Jyväskylän Hill near a Lake' (Ihteinen Jyväskylän mäki järvellä), 1986–87, frozen lake, snow, 1000 × 1000 × 600 cm
This artist, who produced so-called land-art, has changed the environment. He makes us come to terms with a newly constructed horizon. He models huge geometric shapes of a sphere, a parallelogram, or a pyramid.

8

142

The World of Technology

Cars and garages. Creating mobiles. From space research to kitchen utensils. Invisible signals, radio, televison and telephones.

Technology may inspire children's creative activities. After all, some three-year-old children can recognise various makes of cars, and accept unquestioningly phones, computers and videos – which is understandable. However, we can see that technology in our lives should have its limits. For example, cars should not deprive people of their natural inclination to walk; sitting in front of television should not unnecessarily inhibit an individual's creativity. Artists who were the first to admire the rapid impact of technology in our lives very soon began to warn of the dangers involved. They could see that machines seemed to subdue the individual, even though they were invented for his own creature-comforts.

As we all realise that cars, apart from certain advantages, can leave us 'short of breath and exercise' – city children, especially, are aware of pollution – children should be our partners in the following activities. In order to protect the environment let us move cars into underground garages. Even small children are keen to know 'what is inside'. Thus, their drawings look like X-ray

141 *A veteran car.* This drawing is based on a tiny model, a child's toy, placed on a large sheet of paper. Thus, children could see most of it; from the front, from the side, and above. They linked the basic features of the toy, as drawn from different angles, in a strong line. They shaded the drawing in coloured inks and felt-tip pens, and added the fine detail. By drawing hands, the children wanted to show how they played with or repaired their toy cars. We might also suggest that children cut out some interior details of a car or its environment from a magazine and glue them onto their drawing.

142 *A shaded drawing of a car.* Children again used their own toy as a model for this large drawing. This activity might be preceded by drawing the model from four angles, i.e., from one side, from above, from the front, and from the rear.

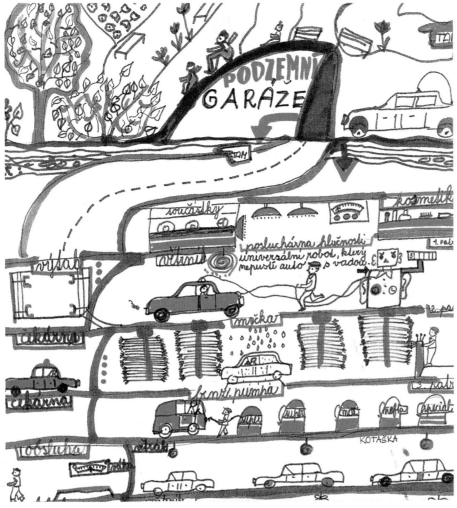

143

143 *Underground garages* drawn in cross-sections of several floors provide children with an opportunity to consider garage equipment and apparatus. In this instance, the children examined a floor complete with a petrol station and car wash. Some children suggested a service station with a practice area for learner drivers. The arrangement of driving simulators, where the less experienced could practise driving on a busy road, was interesting. Moving cars into underground garages also seems to emphasise that city streets should be used by people rather than by their cars.

plates. We might show children technical drawings in order to point out the graphic technique of 'cross-sections'. These are helpful if children attempt fantasy drawings of technical inventions. Children might also try to invent electromobiles for travel in town. Our illustrations provide further suggestions.

If we leaf through popular science-fiction with children, we can see that science and technology advance and, in fact, extend the individual's senses. The individual is able to invent vehicles and vessels in which he can live safely and investigate space or the ocean floor. If the conditions are too hazardous, then robots are used. The so-called 'high-tech' approach is employed in town planning. The house, built in this manner, functions primarily as a machine. Nothing is covered or concealed in terms of its interior or exterior features. One of the best known examples is the Centre Georges Pompidou in Paris, built by Piano and Rogers and opened in 1977.

In myths and legends we can find enough evidence to show small children that humans invented various 'magical' objects in order to 'extend' their senses. Could children name some of them and list their present-day technological equivalents? In fairy tales, which are filled with wisdom and

144 *An electromobile show room.* Although the drawing was based on ordinary cars, the children improved them in order to increase their usefulness in towns. They stressed those parts of a 'mobile' which reflected its value in town. A mobile resembling a vacuum cleaner was designed to absorb dirt and the dangerous pollutants at busy junctions. It would even absorb excessive noise. Another 'machine' functioned as an automatic pavement wiper and polisher. Yet another mobile acted as a 'fountain', spraying pine-scented air-freshener on the streets. In other pictures mobiles appeared as travelling attractions in parks and children's playground areas, acting as small stalls selling balloons and ice-cream; hiring out toys; or as stages for puppet shows. The children drew in coloured felt-tip pens, adding their comments next to the pictures or on the reverse side of the paper. These drawings might represent a catalogue, such as is available at any motor trade-fair.

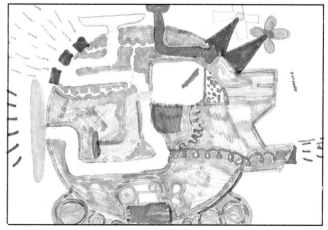

commonsense, magical instruments punish the foolish person and often represent the triumph of good over evil. Younger children might design and illustrate their own fairy tales using common objects which they can convert

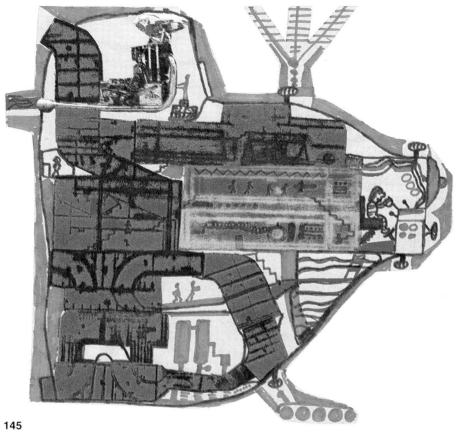

145 *A space laboratory* was made using suitable rubbings, which were completed by drawing in details. In a cross-section of a fantastic spaceship children created a separate control and research area complete with equipment and living quarters for its astronauts.

146 *A space pilot's wardrobe* is a modification of a doll's wardrobe. For once boys will also be keen to take part. The children borrowed from science fiction in order to find inspiration for the astronaut's outfit. Firstly, they drew the figure of the astronaut without his space suit, and cut this out. They then drew several outlines of his body on coloured papers. Afterwards it was a simple task to design space outfits within these shapes, and to cut them out.

145

146

147 *A robot: Cybernetic Granny.* A coloured rubbing was the basis for the construction of a robot. Children made this rubbing from the uneven surfaces of flat metal objects, such as graters and gratings. They then drew a robot whose bodily structure resembled a human body. The children decided on a Cybernetic Granny because they had seen a puppet film of the same name by J. Trnka, the famous Czech film director. In the film, a little girl has two Grannies. One Granny is real, her pockets full of fairy tales and apples. The second Granny is cybernetic, and plans the girl's daily programme – her chores and leisure time, too. Both Grannies call the girl 'Dear'. However, only one of them truly loves her. The girl likes to spend time only with this Granny.

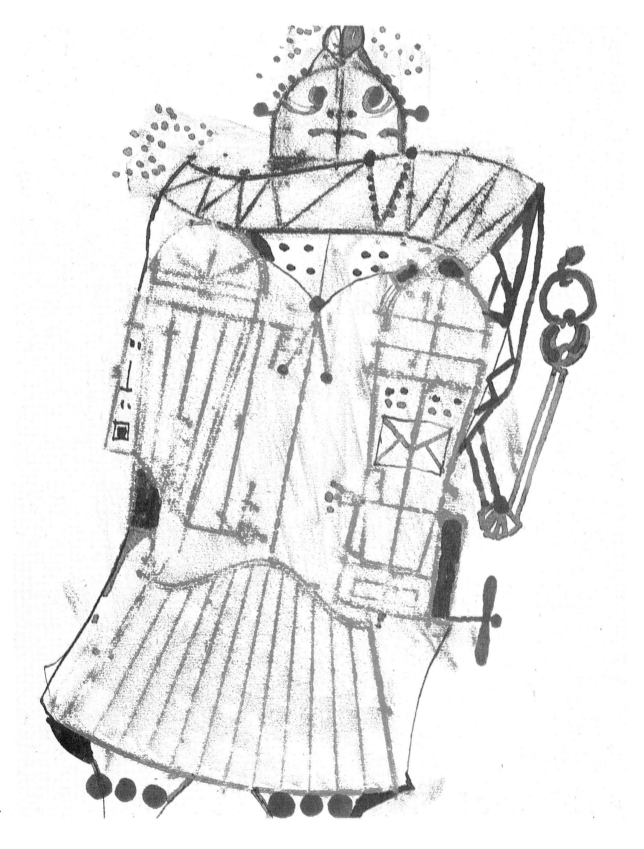

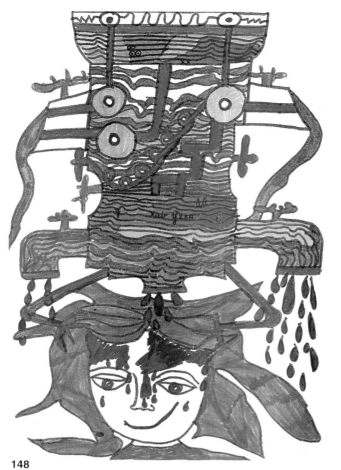

148

149

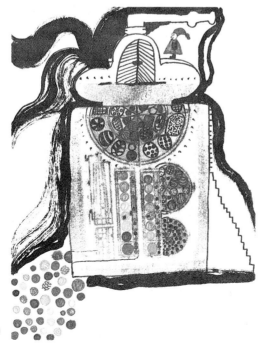

150

148, 149, 150 *Different grinders.* These illustrations were made as rubbings and completed in drawings, shaded drawings in coloured inks, or drawings in Indian ink. Grinders and blenders, found in the kitchen, served as models for drawing the basic shape. The children completed them as 'laboratories' which might produce marbles, sweets, different types of weather, or dreams to order. Some special grinders were visualised as helmets, which might give extra tuition in, e.g. maths, while the wearer was asleep.

Labels within the illustration: SKOŘÁPKY, POTRAVA, BÍLKY ŽLOUTKY, ŽIVÁ KUŘATA, 10038, ODPAD, POJÍZDNÁ SNÁŠÍRNA

151

151 *A mechanical hen in cross-section.* In this illustration children enthusiastically constructed the cross-section of 'an egg farm'. They were amused by this fantasy. Battery hens or broiler chickens lead rather miserable existences. Nevertheless, no robot can ever replace them.

into 'magical' ones. For example, blenders or grinders, found in the kitchen, might provide some inspiration. If we let children examine their internal construction, then they might discover that these utensils resemble little 'factories' which can handle and produce anything – thanks to children's imagination.

We have already realised that the uncritical admiration of technology has its dangers. If children have read Hans Christian Andersen's *The Emperor's Nightingale,* they may well understand why a perfect mechanical toy was not able to bring back the Emperor's health whereas a humble nightingale could. No toy whatsoever can be a substitute for contact with living animals. If we place a fully automated model of a puppy alongside the identical living one in front of a child, it is easy to predict that the child will cuddle and transfer his affections to the latter. It is sometimes hard to understand the popularity of many plastic products, such as artificial grass, artificial flowers and artificial logs in fireplaces.

Let us try to penetrate the surface of reality more deeply. Let us ask the children to draw that which is 'invisible' and yet exists around them. Radio or television waves, impulses of telephone conversations, satellite signals – these channels of communication, human voices, sounds or pictures – all

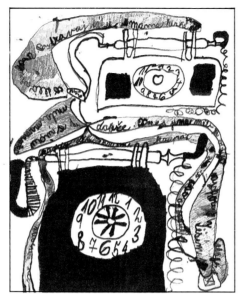

152

153

154

152 *How a 'television cat' went round the world.* Do you remember the Cheshire cat from *Alice's Adventures in Wonderland?* He suddenly appeared in front of Alice, and just as suddenly disappeared again to the top of a tree. Children similarly imagined the appearance of their cat on a television screen. Firstly, they lightly pencilled in the cat's outline. They then drew horizontal lines with a brush. These slightly reminded them of a television's flickering lines. The lines became thicker where they met the outline of the cat.

153 *Phoning Mum.* Even small children can manage to draw the 'conversation' between two telephones. The children usually know what a telephone receiver looks like, or if they are not sure they can have the original in front of them. This activity does not involve drawing the telephone receiver only. It is concerned with capturing a conversation between two people. What is really happening in the wires which transmit the conversation? The children attempted to express the words in symbols, by different colours, or simply by text coloured in between the wires.

154 *The one-man band* reminds us more of a circus clown than a musician. This illustration is rather overstated. The children came back from a concert, and gradually recalled all the musical instruments in the orchestra. Could these instruments be joined together in such a manner that one person could play them using his hands, his mouth, and even his legs? After all, the music was composed by a single person, the composer, who had to imagine the total effect of the individual instruments. Music also affects its listener as a whole.

155 *Signals flying round the Earth.* The children first looked in colour magazines for cut-outs. Using the pictures of oceans, deserts, mountains and forests they created an image of the Earth. Had the children attempted to visualise all the signals that move round the Earth, it would have disappeared – it would have looked more like a ball of thread. Therefore, the children decided to draw only some of these signals. They expressed them in various lines, with signs and codes to differentiate them.

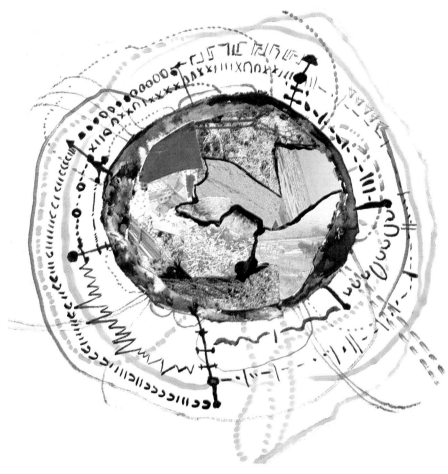

155

When creating a horizontal line with a round brush (picture 152) it is important for children to be able to dip the brush in such a way that it makes an uninterrupted continuous line. The hand and the brush are turned in the direction of the line – as demonstrated in the photograph. Fine lines are created by the tip of the brush as pressure is released; for thick lines pressure is applied.

exist without us observing them. The atmosphere is full of signals, which squeeze past us in streets and pass through our walls. How is it that our telephone conversation can be transformed into an electrical signal and then be transmitted by such thin wires? Recent developments in lasers and fibre-optics enable thousands of conversations to be transferred simultaneously. How is it that an orchestral concert reaches our radio through quiet streets, and the sounds of the many different instruments do not become mingled? Before children learn more about these phenomena in physics lessons, would it not be worthwhile to consider them creatively?

How should we end this chapter? We might perhaps say that the artist is as curious as the scientist – Leonardo da Vinci is the classic example of an enquiring mind. It is interesting to note that Albert Einstein said that imagination was more valuable than knowledge. We might also devote time to another thought of Einstein's: 'Mysteries evoke the best emotions and feelings. These stand at the very cradle of true art and true science. The person who is not aware of such a feeling of mystery, and is not able to observe and be amazed, is virtually dead. He is like a snuffed-out candle.'

Children who possess natural curiosity are able to use their vision and imagination creatively in order to understand the world around them.

A

B

A Vratislav K. Novák (b. 1942)
'Cyclot-dragster', 1987–88, varnished steel,
brass, 18 × 20 × 35 cm
The subtle shape of a very light mobile suggests
a link between human fantasy and play and the
constructive and technological skills of the human brain.

B Aleš Veselý (b. 1935)
'A large compass design', 1984, drawing in
Indian ink and pen, 31 × 46 cm

C Aleš Veselý (b. 1935)
'Tension', 1974–78, scuplture, wood, metal,
height 80 cm
Both works of art are in their content and form
contrary to the subtle *Cyclot*. The artist exa-
mines the forces concealed within huge 'machines' – i.e., tension, traction, weight, the
pressure of bolts and springs – in his sketches
and smaller models of monumental steel sculptures which he later creates. We can anticipate
the concealed rattle and squeaks; even the
strong voice of a variously tuned 'instrument';
the staggering salvo of vibrating metal in this
huge, apparently still sculpture. We admire the
grandeur of an individual's creation, while we
are simultaneously frightened by this irrational
monster.

156

9

157

Handwriting

The communicative and creative value of handwriting. Handwriting reveals personality. Discussions. Lively letters. Letter and number formation. Playing with symmetry. Alphabets and signs.

156 *A page from a wizard's book of spells.* The mysterious shapes of letters, and the way they are joined, resemble magical charms and spells. It looks as if the wizard dictated the text to his cat! The cat wrote with a block of wood held in one of his paws, while taking a stroll across the paper.

157 *Hunting for letters.* Who can 'hunt down' the greatest number of letters and letter types? Children can observe various letter shapes in the accompanying collage – i.e., the proportion of the breadth to the length of a letter; the breadth of a letter mark; various 'serifs' of a letter; colour toning. Could children add at least three other letters of the alphabet to each type of letter illustrated?

From the very beginning of this chapter we should accept that, hard as we may try, some children may not succeed in perfecting their handwriting style. We are only too aware that some children are unable to execute accurate technological drawings or drawings from a model. Handwriting does not only mediate a certain message, and it is not merely a means of recording speech sounds. Handwriting can become a 'work of art' in its creative or expressive form. Children might acquire a deeper appreciation of the beauty and scale of letters if they are involved in enjoyable artistic activities. Children can discover the secrets of letters as signs through their imaginative fantasies. So this chapter deals with two connected levels: firstly, playing with letters from an artistic rather than a communicative point of view; secondly, handwriting linked to a subjective drawing where the communicative value of letters is stressed. Letters on paper must be viewed as having a creative potential of their own.

Handwriting does not only capture the contents of a message, its form also

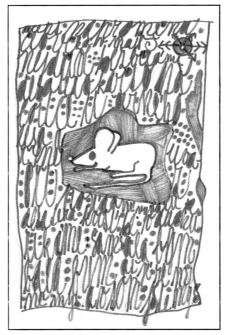

158

159

158 *Cat-and-mouse conversation.* Firstly, the children drew a cat and a mouse. They then filled the rest of the paper with the written text of their conversation. The various shapes of letters express how the stronger animal speaks, and how timidly the weaker one responds. The writing itself is clearly of artistic value, and represents the varied content of the conversation.

159 *A letter from a little mouse.* The children imagined how a little mouse moves, and on the basis of this they decided what its writing might look like.

enables us to recognise the individuality of a person, even down to his or her mood or intentions. Just as two people differ in their appearances and personalities, so their handwriting varies also. In creative play it is possible to reproduce happy handwriting as if formed by a clown in between somersault-

160

161

160 *A monologue of a 'Morse Code' elf.* Most children are familiar with Morse Code dots and dashes. In the illustration, the children attempted to write down in coloured felt-tip pens a story told by this magic elf. The writing is primarily of artistic value – its communicative value is less significant.

161 *A clown's portrait in writing.* In this illustration the shapes of letters also characterise a figure. The children first recalled some well-known fairy tale characters, and made their pencil drawing. They then wrote on the outlines of these portraits what sort of people they depicted, and what their various moods were. The children attempted to adapt the shapes of letters to the characteristics of fairy tale personalities.

162 *Two owls in conversation.* Here the children recorded the hooting of two owls with a black line made by a brush on a sheet of paper. They also created a tone reminiscent of a forest at night. It is very well possible that a certain sound evokes a certain colour image.

162

ing, or a tiny mouse tiptoeing across the paper. Let us go back to Chapter Two and note what moods were expressed by the lines. As two lines might 'hold a conversation' with one another, so two people might do exactly the same by the different characteristics of their handwriting. One written text might be timid or sad. Another text might be angry or aggressive in tone. Children could, for example, attempt to write down their name several times and express by means of the letter shapes the different moods that they are in, e.g., happy, sad, worried, angry . . .

In every language there are some onomatopoeic words. We often imitate people and animals or the tones of instruments and other sounds around us by repeating certain sounds resembling those associated with them. Ask the children to write down the word 'shhh' which is associated with quiet, and the words 'bow-wow' which are full of noise; also, the words resembling a cock

163

163 *Wind and wave talk.* The children interpreted their vision of the undulating movement of the wind and waves in the curved shapes of the letters of the word 'wind'. They also repeated individual letters on the paper. The colour tone used by the children in the illustration corresponds to their notion of these natural elements.

164

crowing and a chick chirping in various letter shapes. Children might produce different letter shapes for these two sentences: 'The wind is murmuring in the tree tops', and 'Suddenly there was a loud rumble of thunder'.

It is a long way from a simple sign (an arrow pointing in a certain direction) through a pictorial symbol to the formation of a letter. However, many stages of this evolution have remained with us. If we draw an arrow in order to indicate a direction, then we talk about a 'mnemogram'. If we see a simplified picture of a pram or a bus, we recognise that it denotes the space reserved for prams

164 *A children's book jacket.* The children first designed the reverse side of the jacket. They practised different type-styles in coloured felt-tip pens as an improvisation, without first drawing them in pencil. The children then imagined each letter as if it were hollow, meaning they had to trace their shapes. Even though they were drawing the letters free-hand, they could always check their proper shape on a template. They selected a simplified animal shape and completed the front cover jacket with letters.

165 *Letters – pictures.* Each letter of the alphabet can, by its shape, remind us of an object, an animal, or even a person. The children attempted to create an entire 'animated' alphabet. This might amuse younger children, still unfamiliar with the alphabet, and even assist them to remember it more easily.

165   **166**

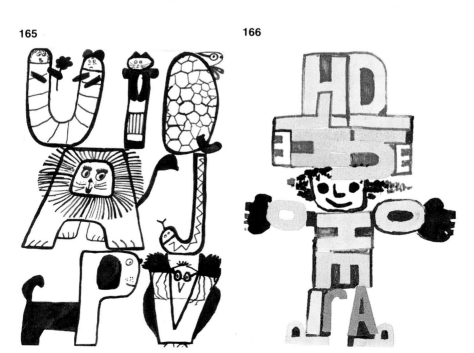

166 *Who escaped from a hoarding?* The children improvised a figure from cut-out letters. They then added suitable detail with a brush.

167 *My friendly computer*. Firstly, the children used a piece of paper folded in half to draw the basic symmetrical shape of a 'computer' – i.e., the figure of a little robot – which they cut out. They created a colour block of rectangles with numerals in the centre of the robot's body. They put each numeral into two equal circles placed one above the other. This task was made easier by using buttons as templates. See the picture below.

167

– this is a 'pictogram', which is understood internationally. However, when an ancient Egyptian drew a snake, and this pictorial sign was associated with its *word meaning* – it meant a 'snake' – this became an 'ideogram'. If we express one speech sound by one letter, this is a 'phoneme'. You might not be aware that a wavy letter 'N' (a phoneme) looked like a wavy cobra in its ancient Egyptian ideogram. The evolution of the alphabet has been complex, and not every letter has its origin in a picture, i.e., in an ideogram. Children might imagine that 'O' is the shape of the sun, a ring or an apple; 'A' could be the

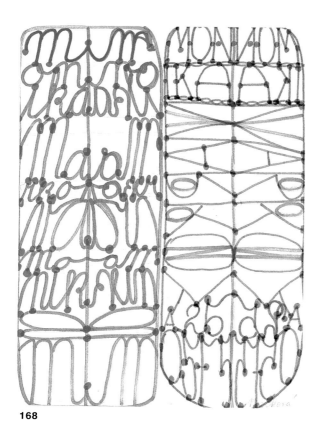

168

169

shape of a bell, a tent or a pyramid. They can begin with capital letters. A more advanced exercise would be to draw letters on graph paper. These could subsequently be cut out and used in collages.

We should not neglect numerals which pre-dated the development of letters. On some clocks there are Roman numerals, which are, in fact, letters. Our numerals are Arabic numerals. Although originating in India, they were introduced into the Western world by the Arabs. We could not imagine a pocket calculator without flashing numbers. Let children draw a calculator in a humorous or whimsical manner, imagining what is going on inside. Children

168 *Barred gates.* Children folded a piece of paper along its vertical axis, and drew the basic symmetrical outline of gates. They then pencilled in the horizontal (random) and vertical (symmetrical) divisions of both sections of the gates. This resulted in the appearance of additional rectangles. On the left-hand section the children designed joined letters. On the right-hand section they attempted the mirror image of the letters.

169 *A totem-pole.* This composition is similar to the 'gates'. Instead of linear writing, the children used the flat type of letters familiar to them from their previous activities.

170

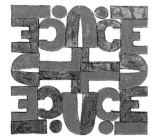 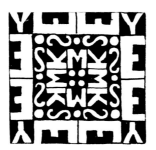 

170 *A scarf design.* The square is the basic shape used in this illustration. Letters are arranged according to the so-called middle diagonals. The children also drew a preliminary net design first. In this instance the net is symmetrical along both axes. The children created the shapes of flat letters, starting at the centre.

171 *Order and chaos*. The children selected and drew a fairly 'quiet' letter, and cut it out. Firstly, the children tried to arrange it in such a manner that its repeated shape would evoke feelings of tranquillity, balance and order. Secondly, the same letter was arranged in such a manner that its repetition would give the impression of restlessness and chaos.

A simple net-lettering template conceals within itself nearly all the letters, whose proportions are three sections in breadth and five sections in length. The template also includes two large and two small circles for the circular letters. Flat letters have their 'mark' one section wide only. The letter 'M' is the only letter of equal proportions (5:5).

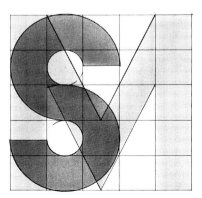

171

should write numbers neatly in order to show respect for them. It will be easier if they use a handful of differently sized buttons as a template.

For creative activities we might offer children letter shapes, handwritten or printed, which they can arrange as decorative elements in a symmetrical pattern. Many possible variations exist. Arranging letter shapes as two doors of a garage, letter 'totems', or square scarf designs could be attempted. Children gradually learn the secret of composition and at the same time they come to appreciate letter proportions and shapes. If we happen to have cut-out letters from a newspaper, children might try similar compositions in collage.

We will leave the production of 'propaganda graphics', i.e., posters, to the experts as it is a very demanding branch of creative art. However, it is valuable for children to observe an advertising hoarding and to consider the creative

172

172 *A naughty letter.* The children first looked at some Japanese and Chinese characters, and tried to classify them into 'pleasant', 'threatening', 'naughty', 'wild', and 'happy' types. They then tried to draw their own imagined characters, which would signify entire words for certain events. Does the character in the illustration remind you of lightning at night?

techniques employed. This can be achieved by comparing several posters. In order to make children's appreciation greater we could ask such questions as: Which poster has the greatest impact at a distance? Which poster seems to say the least? Which poster relies most on lettering for its impact? How many different types of writing can you identify on the poster? Children can also classify motifs: Can you see animals, plants or other objects on these posters? Are they in the form of montage; are they painted; or are they drawn? Children might also prepare a simple paper viewfinder and discover on the

173

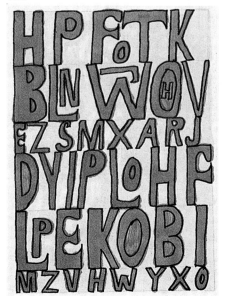

174

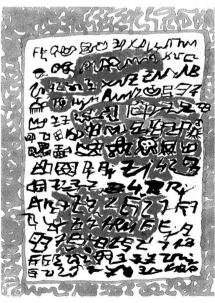

173 *A festive alphabet* is an attempt to create one's own improvised letters, all of which would be expressed in the same style, and would establish a unified design on a sheet of paper. The design is also unified by its colour tone, and the filling in of some letters.

174 *Secret writing* is hugely enjoyable and creative for children. In this instance they drew with a brush dipped in Indian ink. They attempted to write evenly on the whole page, giving it a unified appearance throughout their secret text.

175, 176 *Secret codes using circles in squares* were drawn into a net of squares prepared in advance. The children were asked to complete these particular squares using different circles. As in our own alphabet, repetitions were not allowed.

175

same hoarding smaller compositions consisting of several letters, different motifs, or colour schemes of individual posters. A good poster is always able to draw attention to itself – be it by means of a pun, a simple idea, or the unity of lettering and a motif.

The characters used in Japanese and Chinese writing are aesthetically very valuable. As Europeans we admire not only the lightness of lines drawn by brush but also the artistic abilities and the style of each individual writer. (Some enthusiastic admirers even use Japanese printed materials as wallpaper.) It is not surprising that the shape of Japanese characters has been an inspiration for Japanese calligraphers' creative work. A European who writes in Roman letters cannot share the Japanese calligrapher's experience of

176

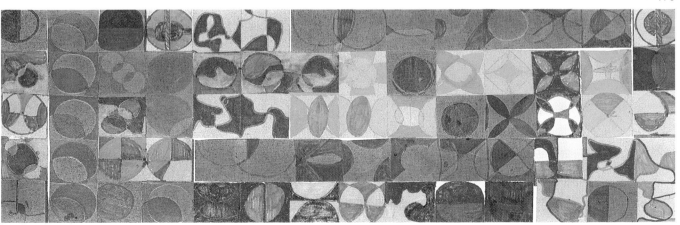

177

producing the shape of a deeply felt character in a broad sweep of his brush on a large canvas. However, we should recall our earlier experiments with a brush or a sponge drawn lightly and rapidly over a sheet of paper (Chapters One and Two). Let us select the initial letter of the word 'wind' (or lightning, anger, bird) and concentrate hard on the whole meaning of that particular word. Only then do we trace the shape of the initial letter in the air, not on paper, but by a gesture. Later, the children might like to practise this activity using a sponge on a large vertical sheet of paper.

Some types of lettering (table on page 125) strike us as a means of writing down secret information. Leonardo da Vinci wrote his diaries in a mirror-writing form, i.e. from the right to the left. (This is said to be easier for left-handed people.) Secret ciphers do exist, and are dealt with by a branch of science called cryptography (from the Greek meaning 'secret writing').

Let us turn now from free handwriting to geometry. Our example of secret

177 *Revelations of a park wall.* Children imagined an old wall, with plaster peeling off, on which words and messages appear, or pictures are drawn. The rain repeatedly lashes the wall, but some of the original messages remain. In this instance, the children drew and wrote on a wet piece of paper, whose tone they had prepared in advance. They then washed their 'wall' under a tap. Some children repeated this activity several times using the same piece of paper.

178

178 *Revelations of an old hoarding.* This illustration was done using the technique of 'de-collage'. Children glued several small posters and magazine cut-outs on top of one another, using a very thin glue. They re-enacted the way in which real posters accumulate on hoardings. However, every hoarding has to be scraped clean from time to time. The children attempted to do this. They did not completely remove every layer. Thus, curious pieces of information and various remnants of lettering and faces remained.

writing on page 121 might remind you of a tiled decorative wall, but it is, in reality, a secret alphabet. Every square contains a different circle which equals one particular letter. The idea of executing a secret alphabet in squares was influenced by the International Flag Alphabet. The flags are, however, designed more distinctly in order that they will be visible on a distant ship's mast. They are not ciphers.

This chapter ends with two illustrations which were produced differently but which nevertheless have certain similarities. In the first illustration the rain repeatedly lashed notices on a wall. In the second illustration layers of posters were torn from a hoarding. In both cases incomplete messages spontaneously appeared. These might remind us of amusing or serious snatches of conversations overheard in the street.

Children encounter writing at every stage of their lives. Let us encourage them to appreciate writing from both artistic and communicative viewpoints.

A Sekidjin Kanó (b. 1924) *'Frenzy'*, 1982, calligraphy in Indian ink on paper, 68 × 138 cm
The artist created a character depicting the human state of mind with a deeply felt single stroke of his brush. According to his statement, this work portrays an individual's fury at his impotence to do anything about the injustice and absurd ways of our world, from wars to nuclear testing. Let us remind children of 'A Naughty Letter' in this chapter, and of the feelings expressed in drawing, referred to in Chapter Two. Thus, free-style calligraphy involves a character and mood simultaneously.

B *Insects* such as a beetle, a grasshopper, or a locust can remind us of a character or a letter. What message does a beetle crawling up and down a tree write? What message does a water-beetle write on the surface of the water?

C *A stone* with its random structure might remind us of the ancient Celtic writing system which recorded messages as arrow-cuts, or the mystic runes used by ancient North Germanic tribes in the 3rd and 4th centuries, and subsesquently by the Vikings.

D *A chart* with several examples of the numerous writing systems created by mankind.
1 Babylonian cuneiform writing
2 Ancient Chinese calligraphy
3 Contemporary printed Arabic writing
4 The Central American Mayan writing system
5 Old Germanic runes
6 Egyptian hieroglyphs
7 Historical decorative Arabic script written with a brush
8 Ancient Indian script
9 Contemporary Japanese poster writing

You might ask children which tool would enable them to most easily write the individual examples shown above (printer's block, brush, block of wood, or pen?)
How do the individual examples affect the children? Do they remind them of, for example, bird's prints /1/, an angry person's gestures /2/, machine parts /3/, recordings of songs or dances /7/, a chicken's dance or a cuckoo's call /8/?

B

C

D

1 2 3

4 5 6

7 8 9